YOU TOO CAN UNDERSTAND THE BIBLE

Matthew

Victor H. Dindot

YOU TOO CAN UNDERSTAND THE BIBLE

Cover: Mary Bean

ISBN 0-89536-467-0

PRINTED IN U.S.A.

To my parents,

Hollas and Mabel Dindot

FOREWORD

I take pleasure in introducing this volume by a former student who is now a colleague in ministry. Victor Dindot knows that there is no more exciting and important endeavor than to appropriate the biblical word for the living of these days. The present volume is evidence of how a pastor can lead others in a study of the Gospel according to Matthew.

There are many commentaries. The author has not attempted to duplicate the various commentaries or simply add to their number. Rather, he has sought to encourage a sustained reading of this Gospel by introducing each section of the Gospel with comments that serve to stimulate group discussion and personal response. The style is simple and direct — avoiding technical terminology. The volume is an invitation to consider the claims of Christian discipleship as these emerge through a study of the Gospel. The reader need not agree in every instance with the author's interpretation. The interpretive comments are intended to stimulate further reflection and appropriation. They point to the Gospel itself. That is how the "then and there" of the biblical word become the "here and now" of our discipleship today.

John F. Jansen
Professor of New Testament
Interpretation
Austin Presbyterian Theological
Seminary

PREFACE

The Bible has remained the best selling book in the world for many centuries. Translations have been made in over one thousand languages and tongues. Almost every home has a copy of the Scriptures lying somewhere on a shelf or a table. In recent years, new versions have been produced which are written in up-to-date language — one is paraphrased so that readers can understand difficult biblical thoughts and expressions.

However, the amount of Bible reading done by many who possess a copy is dangerously low. Thousands of Bibles collect dust and many pages never see the light of day. The chief reason for this situation is that many do not understand what they are reading. They do not comprehend it because it was written many centuries ago by men who lived in a completely different world. Polls taken recently demonstrate that a low percentage of people in the United States have any grasp of the Bible — its stories and message.

In order to understand the Bible, it is necessary to have some kind of commentary to go with it. Merely sitting down and reading the Bible — no matter how simple the version — is not enough. There are too many ideas and customs presented in its pages that need some explanation for modern readers.

There are many commentaries written by outstanding and competent biblical scholars. However, a large portion of them are written for other scholars and ministers; a few are designed for lay people; none exist — that I know of — for Senior Highs or younger. I have heard some say that some commentaries were harder to understand than the Bible itself.

This book is my attempt to help others understand better the meaning of the Bible by providing a commentary that employs thoughts and language that anyone, hopefully, can understand. I have tried to avoid all technical language that might drive the reader to a dictionary.

It is my hope and prayer that anyone who reads it — even young people, college age and younger — will be helped in some small way by this book. The Gospel of Jesus Christ is for everyone. It must be understood before it can take hold of us.

For whatever value this book may have, I must make some acknowledgments. I am grateful to all of the members of the congregations I have served, and to those who encouraged me to write. With appreciation I acknowledge the help I received from Mrs. Blanche Piper, an author of two books and a member of the Presbyterian Church of Adamsville, Texas, which I also serve. I am especially grateful to my former professor and constant friend, Dr. John F. Jansen, Professor of New Testament Interpretation at Austin Presbyterian Theological Seminary, who encouraged me to go through with this project and has helped immensely by his great interest and keen criticism. He has also written the Foreword for this book.

Victor Dindot

Introduction to Matthew

Matthew, Mark, Luke, and, John did not give us a story of the life of Jesus. Instead, they wrote down many of his sayings and teachings, and recorded some of the events which took place during the last three years of his life on earth. Only Matthew and Luke give us any details about the birth of Jesus; Luke is the only writer who tells about an event in the life of Jesus when he was twelve years old.

Their purpose is the same: to prove that Jesus is the Christ, the Son of God. By believing and trusting in Jesus Christ, people come into the right relationship to God.

Matthew wrote his Gospel (meaning "good news" or "glad tidings") for Jewish Christians who needed to defend themselves against the Jews who had not accepted Jesus as God's Son, and who often criticized these converts for their beliefs about Jesus. Matthew's aim is to tell the Jews that Jesus is their true king.

Members of the Jewish nation were descendants of Abraham, who had lived twenty centuries before the time of Jesus. God had promised him that all of his descendants would be blessed, that they would possess their own land, and that they would receive God's protection. The people were to do their part by obeying God and by revealing him to other nations. However, history shows that they failed to live up to their responsibilities. They broke his laws, worshiped false gods, and often forgot him. Because of their continued disobedience, God allowed two nations to take them into captivity.

Ten of the twelve tribes of Israel were conquered and taken away from their land by the nation of Assyria in 722 B.C. In 587 B.C., the two remaining tribes, Judah and Benjamin, were taken into captivity by the Babylonians. Years later the people of these two tribes were allowed to return to their homeland. Even after their hard lesson they still did not love and obey God the way God had intended. The members of the Jewish nation became self-centered: they separated themselves from the rest of the world, stressed their Jewish identity, and attempted to live their lives according to the Law. By doing this they ignored the commission of God: that they should go out into the world and win the Gentiles (anyone not a Jew) to obedience and faith in the one true God. The Jews emphasized those things which distinguished them from others and thought mainly of their own glory and preservation.

For many years the Israelites looked for a Messiah (meaning a "king who would rule the people" or "anointed one"). The word "Christ" in Greek is the same as the Hebrew "Messiah." Matthew wrote his Gospel to tell the people that Jesus is the Christ, the Messiah. He quotes from the Old Testament many times to prove to the Jewish people that Jesus was the one for whom they had been looking.

God sent Jesus at the right time in world history. Conditions were right for the spread of the message of the Gospel. Rome controlled most of the known world and there was peace, making it safe to travel on the good roads which the Empire had built.

Jesus' Ancestry

Matthew 1:1-17

All of us have ancestors — our parents, our grandparents, great-grandparents, and on back many generations. We may have an ancestor who was a soldier in the Revolutionary War. One, two, or more ancestors might have been well known many years ago. There also might be some we would rather not know too much about.

Jesus had some famous ancestors in his family tree like Abraham and David. Some are not well known such as Satathiel or Elioud. It is not as important to know who our ancestors were as it is to discover who we are and what we are.

But to the Jews it was important to have a record of the family tree to prove that a person was a Jew. So Matthew begins his story with the record of Jesus' ancestors. There were no books for the people to read, so everyone had to depend upon his memory. To make it easier to remember, Matthew divides the list into three sections of fourteen generations.

The first section takes the story from Abraham to David; the second from David to the exile in Babylon; and the third to Jesus Christ.

The language of the Old Testament does not have vowels like our English. They did not have numbers like one, two, and three.

Each letter of their alphabet was given a number value. The name for David was DWD, D=four, W=six. Add the three letters and it adds up to fourteen.

The record was meant to prove that Jesus was the son of David. It was easier to learn it and memorize it by this method.

The Engagement
Matthew 1:18-25

This story puzzles us because we don't understand why Joseph would want to divorce Mary if they were only betrothed. The reason for this is that marriage customs in Jesus' time were different from ours.

A man and woman were often engaged to be married when they were children. It was like a promise made that they would be married when they grew up. Often the parents were responsible for the engagement of their son or daughter. Many times the engagement was made without the couple seeing each other.

Then there was the betrothal. This lasted for a year before the actual marriage. During that time they were known as man and wife, and the only way to break the relationship was to get a divorce.

After one year there was the marriage itself. Joseph and Mary had not yet become married. Since Mary was pregnant and Joseph did not want her to have a bad reputation, he decided to divorce her secretly. He hoped to avoid a scandal as much as possible.

While he was planning to do this, he was told in a dream not to worry. A great miracle had taken place: a son would be born to them who would change lives and bring people back to God. The Holy Spirit had conceived a child in Mary who would be named Jesus. "Jesus" means "God is salvation." "Joshua" is the Hebrew name for the Greek "Jesus."

The Wise Men
Matthew 2:1-12

Bethlehem was the birthplace and home of the great King David. The people believed that the Messiah would come from the line of David, and he would be born in his home town. Jesus was born in Bethlehem which was built on the side of a hill. There were many caves of limestone where the town was located. It is very likely that Jesus was born in one of these caves, rather than in a barn or shed.

The wise men were highly educated in the knowledge of their time. In those days most everyone believed in astrology. They believed they could see into the future by studying the stars. The stars were dependable; they always stayed on the same course. But if a bright star suddenly appeared, then this meant that God was changing his own order in the universe and was announcing a great event.

We do know that some stars appeared brighter than usual about the time Jesus was born, but we do not know which one the wise men followed. Some star told them that something great was about to happen, so they followed it.

We have always thought that there were three wise men. Matthew does not tell us how many there were; he simply mentions the three gifts given to Jesus. More than likely there were more than three men who made the long journey. The deserts were dangerous places for long distance traveling. There were wild animals and, worse, many robbers waited for someone to come along. Three wealthy men traveling many miles through deserted places would not have reached their destination without running into trouble. How many there were we do not know, but there must have been more than three who came from the East to honor Jesus.

When Herod the Great heard about the birth of a king from the wise men, he became upset. Since he had the title of "king," he believed that this young child was a threat to his throne.

Herod was not all bad as king of the Jewish nation. He was the only ruler who had kept peace in the land. He ordered that the temple be rebuilt for the people. The temple was the great center of worship for the Jews which had first been built by King Solomon eight hundred years before. He had reduced taxes when people could not afford to pay. And he sold some gold to buy grain when many were starving.

But he was extremely suspicious and jealous of others. He constantly suspected that people were plotting against him, so he had many of them murdered, including some of the members of his own family. When he heard about a new king, he plotted to have him eliminated. He gave the impression to the wise men that he would also like to worship him. They did not realize that Herod wanted Jesus killed. A dream revealed to them Herod's true intentions.

Escape to Egypt and Return
Matthew 2:13-23

Two thousand years ago the people of the world believed that God sent messages by means of dreams. Another dream came to Joseph telling him to take his family to Egypt because Herod was going to have all the baby boys in Bethlehem, who were two years old and younger, murdered. They stayed there until it was safe to return.

Israel had regarded Moses as the greatest of all leaders; he had delivered God's Law, the Ten Commandments, to the people at Mount Sinai. Matthew tells us that Jesus is the "new Moses." Like Moses, Jesus escapes death as a baby; he is called out of Egypt; he is tempted in the wilderness like Moses was tempted to bring water from the rock. Jesus gives the new law from the mountain just as Moses gave it from another mountain. The old and the new covenants are both sealed in blood. Jesus is greater than Moses, and his teaching supersedes all other teaching in Israel.

After Herod the Great died, Joseph, Mary, and Jesus returned to their homeland, but instead of going to the town of Bethlehem in Judea in the southern part of Palestine, they went to Nazareth of Galilee in the north. Archelaus, Herod's son and the ruler of Judea, was even more dangerous than his father. Herod Antipas was a better ruler in Galilee.

The second chapter of Matthew ends with Jesus as a little child while the third chapter begins when he was about thirty years old. Only Luke records any event in his life during these years: Jesus visited the temple at the age of twelve.

We do not know what was taking place in Jesus' life during this time. No one has left any information for us to read. However, we can be sure that Jesus was preparing himself for the great task that God had given him: for the three years that he preached, taught, and healed.

John the Baptist

Matthew 3:1-17

Prophecy had died out in the nation of Israel; it had been four hundred years since the last prophet had proclaimed God's word, i.e., what God wanted his people to know. (The Old Testament prophets spoke when the nation of Israel had disobeyed God's laws.)

The people regarded John the Baptist as a prophet — one who spoke for God. He even looked like a prophet, wearing animal skins and eating food he found in the country. He went from place to place speaking against wrong actions and evil. If a person was living his life the wrong way, John would tell him to change his way of living. If he was excluding God from his life, John would tell him to accept God. Wherever he saw evil — in a crowd, in town, or even in the palace of a king — he would condemn it. John was not seen with a smiling face; he was serious. He told the people to turn to God before it was too late. The day of God's judgment was coming. Being a descendant of Abraham did not protect one from God's coming judgment: repentance was the only solution; it must be accompanied by baptism in the river.

When the people were baptized by John, they confessed their sins. (Sin is the breaking of God's laws by thought, word and action, i.e., doing what is displeasing to God.) Repentance is the condition of baptism. "To repent" means simply "to turn." Repentance is turning away from evil and turning to God. When we repent we change our attitude toward God and others. We hate our sins and put them out of our minds, intending never to repeat them. Because we realize that God loves us, we, in turn, love God, knowing that we are dependent on him.

Jesus asked John to baptize him. Jesus had no need to repent of any sin or any wrong, so the reason for Jesus' baptism is puzzling. One idea is that the baptism of Jesus marked the beginning of his mission on earth. He was the Messiah who had come to save the people, but he also came as a servant who obeyed God completely. Both of these ideas are brought together when a voice from heaven proclaimed, "This is my beloved Son, with whom I am well pleased." These words are taken from Psalm 2:7 and Isaiah 42:1.

The Three Temptations
Matthew 4:1-11

How was Jesus going to accomplish his life's work? How was he going to bring people into the right relationship with God? With this on his mind, Jesus went into the desert to think about his strategy, to be alone with his thoughts, and to pray to God.

First came the temptation to change stones into bread. They even looked like loaves on the desert. He could do it, if he so desired. If he could provide bread for the many people who had so little to eat, if he could fill their stomachs, then they would be satisfied and would listen to what he had to say. But this would be bribery. It would mean getting followers on the basis of what they could get out of it. Many would follow him just because they could get something to eat for nothing. So Jesus rejected this method because it would not bring dedicated disciples. It is not the eating of food which makes life worth living; it is the doing of that which God desires of us.

Then Jesus was tempted to do something spectacular. Why not go up on top of the Temple and jump off? It was 450 feet to the ground below, because the Temple was built on the edge of a plateau and there was a valley beneath it. If the people saw this amazing stunt, they would follow him because they would know he had amazing powers. Imagine, defying the law of gravity. Even the Scriptures would support him. "He will put his angels in charge of you and they will hold you up with their hands, in case you hurt your foot against a stone."

But Jesus discarded this method also. People would not believe in him as a savior; they would only follow him because he had done something sensational. Jesus came to give us a new relationship with God; he did not come to show off his powers.

This would also be putting God to the test. It would be forcing God to come to the rescue of Jesus because of a dangerous situation in which Jesus had placed himself. The Israelites had put God to the test out in the desert many years before when they demanded water. Because of this incident, Moses was not allowed to go to the Promised Land (Exodus 17:1-7; Deuteronomy 6:16).

Then comes the temptation to make obeying God a little easier. Do not make it so difficult to become a Christian; lower the standards. After all, people have many weaknesses; they cannot live up to all the demands of the faith. Do not ask people to give everything to God. Let them get away with doing wrong occasionally. Let them follow their selfish desires of wealth, power and position. Make serving God take up less time; make it easier to serve God. God should not expect so much anyway.

But Jesus rejected this way also because he knew the command that all should worship God and him only.

Jesus Returns
Matthew 4:12-17

John the Baptist had been arrested for criticizing Herod, the king. The king had taken his own brother's wife and made her his wife, after he had forced his own wife to leave him. John was not afraid to speak against wrongdoing wherever he saw it.

Jesus went back to Galilee to live, but he did not return to his childhood home, Nazareth. Instead he moved to Capernaum and there he set up his headquarters. He was beginning his work and he needed to begin from a new place.

Galilee was a small country, only fifty miles north to south and half that distance from east to west. But it was a fertile land. Crops and plants seemed to grow in every square of land. Because it was so rich in produce, it was heavily populated. It was said that there were 204 villages and all had a population of 15,000 or more.

Jesus was beginning his work where there were many people to hear him who were willing to listen to new ideas. In Judea the people were too set in their ways and did not accept changes very easily.

Jesus began to preach about the kingdom of God. "Preach" means to proclaim a message from a king.

The Call of the Disciples
Matthew 4:18-22

There were at least nine cities around the Sea of Galilee. It was a crowded area then, with many fishing boats on the water. Jesus had mingled with the men who fished for a living, and he found his first four disciples there. No doubt he talked to them many times, telling them that they would have to give up fishing for fish and go fishing for men. They were to be his assistants, go with him wherever he went, learn what he taught them, and do what he required them to do. It would not be an easy life; they might wish many times that they could go back to fishing.

Fishermen would make good disciples for several reasons. They were patient. They had learned to wait for the fish to catch the bait. In preaching and teaching much patience is required to finally see results. A fisherman cannot be discouraged and he cannot give up. He must always try again when nothing happens. A fisherman must stay out of sight; if he gives himself away the fish won't bite. A disciple must forget his own personal desires. A Christian does not call attention to herself or himself, but rather to God.

Jesus Preaches, Teaches and Heals
Matthew 4:23-25

This short section sums up the work of Jesus' life: (1) preaching — giving the truths of God; (2) teaching — explaining the meaning and the significance of these truths; (3) healing — removal of the agony and pain which hinders a person from realizing his or her capabilities.

The synagogue services were very different from today's church services. There was no minister who spoke from a pulpit every week. Any qualified man could read and make comments on the Scripture during the service. There were only three parts to the service: prayer, reading from the Scriptures, and an address by a man chosen by the president of the synagogue. So Jesus had many opportunities to present the good news of the kingdom of God to those who heard him in the synagogues.

But Jesus also healed; people with all kinds of diseases were brought to him or came to him and were made well. It did not take long for reports to spread around the area. Jesus' popularity was growing at a very fast rate.

More Than Happiness
Matthew 5:1-12

The Sermon on the Mount is a condensation of many of the teachings of Jesus. It is very likely that all the sayings in this section were not spoken by Jesus at one time, but rather were scattered throughout his ministry.

There is significance in Matthew saying that Jesus sat down. It was the custom for rabbis to sit down when their teaching was official. When there was something of major importance to be said, the teacher sat. But when he was merely giving instructions, he might stand up or walk around while he was talking. Here Jesus is giving the right understanding of God's law, so he sits down.

Why isn't the word "happy" found in many translations instead of "blessed"? It is because "happiness" comes from the word "hap" which means "chance" or "luck." Happiness is dependent on circumstances around us. We can be happy one day and unhappy the next, because our happiness depends on what happens to us. But Jesus means "blessed." This is the joy which comes from doing what God desires for us. Because we know we are always doing what God wants, we have an inner joy which does not come and go or depend on what happens to us. We have a permanent happiness which no amount of tragedy or evil can take away.

The poor in spirit are those who realize their spiritual poverty. They have nothing they can brag about but depend completely on God. This does not mean that lacking material things is good; Christians aim to remove that poverty.

Those who mourn. This does not refer to those who grieve over the loss of loved ones; they would not experience joy. "Those who mourn" are the ones who are deeply sorry for their sins and failures. No one can come to God unless he or she is sorry for his or her sins. "The perfect sacrifice is a broken and contrite heart."

The meek. This is an unfortunate translation because it implies one who always gives in, who can be pushed around, who is anemic, weak-willed, and so forth. There are several ways the Greek word can be translated into English. "Blessed are the gentle" might convey the meaning more clearly. These people do not push their weight around; they are not aggressive; they are self-controlled; or better yet, God-controlled. They will inherit God's kingdom.

Those who hunger and thirst for righteousness are those who desperately want to come into a right relationship with God. But they know they cannot do this on their own or by their own willpower. It has to be given to them by God. When God gives them his righteousness, they are satisfied because they have been acquitted of all wrongdoing.

The merciful. God is merciful to us all even though we do not deserve it. If God does this to us, should we do any less? We must forgive others for all the hurtful things they do to us. Jesus taught that we cannot expect mercy from God unless we forgive people for the harm they inflict on us. True forgiveness means more than merely forgetting what has been done to us. It means trying to understand why the person who offended us did what he or she did. If we can put ourselves in that person's place (figuratively), we can better see why that action was taken.

The pure in heart. Many times we do good things for selfish reasons. We give to some good cause because we want to be recognized for doing it. Even when we do our best we are not always free from self-centered motives. The pure in heart do good to please God and not to enhance their own image.

The peacemakers. This beatitude is not meant to apply only to an exclusive group of men who negotiate at meetings during conflicts between nations, hoping to bring peace. People often get on each other's nerves, resulting in rifts between them. People often misunderstand each other and hold ill feelings. The peacemakers are those who work to bring people into harmonious relationships. The peacemakers are also those who work to reconcile people to God. They strive to bring others into a relationship of love towards God, because God has already shown his love to them. The term "sons of" is an adjective which means "God-like" or "children of God."

Those who are persecuted for the sake of Jesus Christ. Because Christians pledge their loyalty to Jesus Christ, there will be times when the faithful will have to suffer ridicule and criticism from those who do not understand Christianity or are hostile towards it. It may mean giving up an opportunity to advance or succeed because the way is hurtful to others. It may mean going against the accepted ways of the group. A Christian is motivated by love. He will often have to suffer scorn because he is not willing to go along with a way that is wrong.

The last beatitude is a restatement of the previous one. It was understood better in Jesus' day than it is now. In our own time we do not suffer greatly for our religious beliefs and practices. However, shortly after Jesus' death and Resurrection Christians were falsely accused of many misdeeds: (1) cannibalism — because Jesus said, "Take, eat, this is my body"; (2) immoral activities — because they met in secret; (3) arson — because they spoke of the world as coming to an end in flames; (4) draft-evaders — because they refused to fight in wars; (5) atheism — because they did not accept Caesar as a god. Many Christians were burned on crosses, or torn in half by being tied between two horses running in different directions. Some were dressed up in animal skins and were attacked by wild dogs. Others were murdered. This beatitude meant much to those who suffered for Jesus Christ.

Salt and the Light
Matthew 5:13-14

Jesus is comparing the Christian to salt. Salt has two qualities. It brings out the flavor of food and it preserves the food by preventing it from spoiling. The Christian faith is not dull, lifeless, unenthusiastic, or boring. True faith is enthusiastic, happy, and positive. It gives flavor to living. Salt prevents food from decay, from going bad. So believers in Christ do not allow the world with all its enticements to influence them. They do not become tarnished or allow themselves to decay; they retain their honesty and integrity. They are also a good influence on others; they prevent others from going bad.

By comparing his followers to light, Jesus is saying that they are to be seen. There is no such thing as a disciple who keeps his or her discipleship a secret. All should know that a person is what he or she claims to be, i.e., one who follows Jesus Christ.

A Better Righteousness
Matthew 5:17-20

The scribes and the Pharisees believed that it was perfectly possible to obey all the laws of God. The way to accomplish this was to take the commandments and make rules and regulations out of them by defining all that a person could and could not do in any situation. The scribes invented all the rules and regulations; the Pharisees (separated ones) cut themselves off from ordinary life so that they could observe the rules. By the third century A.D., these regulations were put into written form called the "Mishnah," a book 800 pages long. Then, in order to explain the "Mishnah," commentaries called "Talmuds" were produced. These commentaries required many volumes to accommodate the thousands of petty rules and regulations. Jesus constantly broke these rules.

Luke 13:10-17 tells about Jesus healing a woman who had had a bent back for many years. This was done on the Sabbath, and immediately he was criticized by the president of the synagogue. The rule stated that a person could only be healed on the Sabbath if it were a matter of life and death. Even a wound could be treated only to prevent it from becoming worse, not to make it better. A bandage could be put on the wound, but no medication. Jesus broke this rule and many others. Helping people was (and is) more important than any rule. Jesus did things which were beneficial to men, women, and children. Any law which prevents one person from helping another is not a good law; it should be abolished. The Ten Commandments were given by God to help us in our relationship to one another and to him. Jesus upheld the commandments of God. He frequently broke the laws made by men.

A Standard Greater Than the Law
Matthew 5:21-48

The religious leaders believed that it was possible to obey God's law completely. If a person did not kill, steal, commit adultery, lie, or want what someone else had, that person could assume the law was being obeyed. But Jesus places before his followers a higher standard which God demands.

Anger is equivalent to murder. If we are angry at someone we are as guilty as someone who takes a life. If we have hatred in our hearts, it means we have the desire to have that person eliminated from our lives. Thinking about it is the same as adultery. Desiring a person of the opposite sex who is married is no better than actually having intimate relations with that person. Lust is just as damaging as the act itself.

Even divorce is classified as being as serious as adultery. God intended for marriage to be a lifetime union of man and woman. In Jesus' day there was a custom that if a man made a statement which was guaranteed to be the truth, he would take an oath using God's name. This was supposed to guarantee the validity of a statement, because God was regarded as a partner in the oath. But Jesus says that taking an oath in this manner is unnecessary; God is already there. On the other hand, it was the custom to avoid using God's name; in fact it was forbidden to speak God's name aloud. So people would swear by "heaven" or by "earth" or by "Jerusalem" or even one's own head. It was pointless to use these terms; a person's word should be good enough. It also eliminates the taking of God's name in vain, i.e., the trivial use of the name of deity.

Jesus was also saying that a Christian does not retaliate for a wrong done to him or her, nor permit a personal insult by others. A person is to be above allowing anyone to disrupt his or her love for others.

The Old Testament never stated that one should hate one's enemy. The practice in Jesus' time was to love only the neighbor, i.e., Jews, and those of the same religious beliefs. The Old Testament commanded love toward members of one's own nationality. Hatred was only justified toward enemies of God.

But Jesus condemned this discriminatory love. Our love should include all, regardless of what we think of them, how unlikable they are, or how they have hurt us. The love Jesus was talking about is not love as we usually understand it. It has nothing to do with romance or even warm feelings toward others. This kind of love means that we want the best for that person; we have goodwill toward him or her; we do what is best for that person, no matter what he or she does to us or thinks about us.

This kind of love is like God's love toward us. We don't deserve his love: we forget God; we disobey God; we often act out of selfish motives; we fail to do his will. Yet God loves us even though we don't merit it. And because God loves us in this unrestricted manner, we should do the same to others. We are to love perfectly as God does.

The Right Motive
Matthew 6:1-4

Jesus was warning his hearers against doing the right things for the wrong reasons. As Christians, we are to give generously of what God has permitted us to have. We are to give in order to support the church; in order to feed and clothe the poor; in order to support the mission work of the church. Our giving should be a matter between God and us. We should not advertise what we give so that others will commend us. Rather, we should give offerings with the idea that only God will know.

Some have maintained that the idea of rewards is not a part of the Christian faith. They say we should do good for the sake of doing good, that the concept of receiving something for what is done is not a part of the gospel. But Jesus clearly stated that God will reward us for what we do from right motives. We cannot be more spiritual than Jesus himself on this matter.

On the other hand, we do not do good deeds for the sole purpose of receiving a reward. We are not to seek out rewards. If we do, we will think of God as a keeper of accounts. We will believe that the more we do the more God will favor us and will shower us with rewards. Instead of giving and doing for others out of love, it becomes a matter of repayment for services rendered. Our motive would be to accumulate for ourselves, rather than to love unselfishly, desiring the best for another.

What rewards can we expect? The rewards may not be material. The reward may be satisfaction, a feeling of well being, a sense of the right relationship to God. The reward may mean more work or greater responsibility. (Remember the parable of the Talents.) It may simply be the joy of serving God.

Real Prayer
Matthew 6:5-6

In the days of Jesus it was the custom among the Jews to pray three times a day, at 9 a.m., 12 noon, and 3 p.m. A man had to stop what he was doing and pray at these times. Many would make sure they were in places where they could be seen by many other people, like at street corners, the city square, etc., so when they prayed, all in the vicinity could see their piety. But Jesus says that prayer is between the individual and God. We do not pray to be heard by others; we are addressing God and him alone. Prayer must not be a matter of clever words, but should come from the heart. We do not pray to impress others; we pray to God who is ready to listen to what is on our minds and in our hearts. God hears every prayer; we do not have to coax or beg. He is not persuaded to act because of a great volume of words; rather we should pray simply, like the prayer that was given the disciples of Jesus.

The Disciples' Prayer
Matthew 6:7-18

This prayer has always been called the Lord's Prayer, but it is not a prayer Jesus would have prayed himself. Since he committed no sin, he would not ask for forgiveness. It is a prayer for disciples, for those who have a relationship with God.

The prayer is divided into two parts. The first part of the prayer pertains to our attitude toward God and his supreme place in the world. There are three of these expressions. The second part is concerned with human needs: the past, the present, and the future. The prayer asks for "bread," which is necessary to maintain life today; then it asks for "forgiveness," for all wrongs in the past; then it places our future in God's hands, asking for help in overcoming "temptation."

"Our Father who art in heaven." Only children can address anyone as "Father." Only those who have placed themselves in a subordinate position to God, recognizing him as their creator and giver of life, are able to say, "Father." Jesus referred to God as "Father" many times. The Gospels record that name over 150 times. If we see God as "Father," then we see all people as brothers and sisters; we see God as being interested in all of our concerns; we see God as loving each person; we see God suffering when we suffer; we see God helping us in times of trouble; and we understand our forgiveness more clearly.

"Hallowed be thy name." We cannot see or touch God, but we know him by his name. Words are symbols of reality. In biblical times a person was equivalent to his or her name. To "hallow" God's name means to make him great, and we do this by trustful obedience to him, demonstrating that we truly believe in him.

"Thy kingdom come, thy will be done, on earth as it is in heaven." Jesus spoke of the kingdom as being in the past, the present, and the future. He said that Abraham, Isaac and Jacob are in the kingdom, that the kingdom of God is within us, and that we should pray for the coming of the kingdom. What is the kingdom? Members of the kingdom are those who do the will of God on earth as God has intended for it to be done. The kingdom exists where people allow God to control and rule their lives. The kingdom is not a geographical location on a map; it is found in the hearts of people.

"Give us this day, our daily bread." This means exactly what it says. We are asking God for the food we need to keep our bodies going and to keep us healthy. If our bodies are weakened by lack of food or improper nutrition, then we will not be able to think clearly or work efficiently. Jesus cured many who were ill. He knew that people cannot use their abilities to their fullest if they are restricted by ill health. This is asking God to grant us a present need. Food, shelter and sleep are essential for the maintenance of life.

"And forgive us our debts as we forgive our debtors." Whenever we sin against God or another person, we are in debt. We owe God and neighbor but we cannot repay. So we ask God to forgive, to remove the debt completely. We can only ask for forgiveness or the removal of the debt if we ourselves have forgiven others for the wrongs, real or imaginary, they have done to us. God will not forgive anyone who is unwilling to forgive others.

"Lead us not into temptation, but deliver us from evil." James, in his letter, says that "God tempts no one." The temptation comes from our own desires to have what does not belong to us or to do what we know is wrong. We realize that we face temptations all the time, and we ask God to be with us in the fight to overcome the actual carrying out of these sinful desires. On the other hand "temptation" can mean "test." God does test us to see if we are faithful to him. We should never think that being a Christian will automatically protect us from all trouble or danger.

"For thine is the kingdom and the power and the glory forever." This was not a part of the original prayer. It was probably added in the second century to keep it from having such an abrupt ending. The prayer begins and ends with God's glory, making our honor of God more important than our needs. The prayer opens and closes with the attention on God. Verse 14 is an explanation of verse 12. Once again Jesus says not to let religious observances become a matter of show.

Ways to Enter His Kingdom

Matthew 6:19-34

Jesus was not condoning irresponsibility in saving up for the future. If we do not attempt to save some of our earnings, we may end up in financial trouble sooner or later. Rather, Jesus was saying that our thoughts and actions should be centered on God and his kingdom. What are the goals of life? What do we really want to acquire? Don't concentrate on material treasures because they do not last; they deteriorate, and they do not bring satisfaction. If we want only money and things, we will discover that the purpose in life is the acquisition of more earthly treasure. We are never satisfied with what we have; we want a greater amount.

Jesus warned us against aiming for things that can wear out (are eaten by moths or rust away), or that can be stolen (valuable objects or money). These treasures are only temporary; we cannot hold onto them for very long; they lose their importance and value easily. Besides, we must leave them behind when we leave this world and enter the next one.

The treasures that Jesus referred to are spiritual. They are the treasures that we store up for ourselves in God's kingdom. God will give us the treasures which have been stored up for us when it is time for them to be revealed.

The "sound eye" means that we focus on the things of God. When we direct our sights toward God, all earthly matters are placed in the proper light. We see clearly what is trivial and unimportant in this world and have a vision of God's expectations for us. Light is associated with goodness and darkness with evil.

A "master" is one who demands absolute obedience from one who serves him. He claims exclusive ownership. What he wants done must be carried out by the servant. It is obvious that we cannot serve two masters. No one can devote his or her life to two, if either one demands complete submission. It would be impossible. Even more impossible would be to belong to two masters who are at cross-purposes. If God is the master of our lives, then material things can claim no mastery over us. If we are controlled by worldly goods, then we cannot serve God. Being a Christian is a full-time experience. We can serve only one master; the rest must go.

If God can care for and provide that which is necessary for the lives of even birds and plants, then he can certainly give us what is essential for our lives. It is futile and a waste of time to become worried about what we will eat or wear. It will not change conditions around us, worry will only wear us down. Worry is an indicator of a lack of faith in God's providence. By worry we limit God in our own minds. We can expect trouble to occur, but if we are trying to do God's will we must trust him to see us through our troubles. We are not to magnify our troubles by imagining what might happen tomorrow.

Things usually do not turn out the way we think they will.

Worrying about what will happen tomorrow hinders us from trusting God. Jesus is not saying we only have to sit back and let God do it all. He is not telling us not to work. The birds get the worms, but God does not throw them in the nests.

We must do all we can and leave what we cannot do to our heavenly Father. Besides, worry can have a damaging effect on our minds and bodies.

Two Warnings
Matthew 7:1-6

These verses should change a lot of misconceptions about judgment. We will be judged by the way we judge others. We are all guilty of this; we are usually more severe in our judgments of others than necessary. The record of history has shown that so many misjudgments have been made, that it should remind us never to judge others. Many great pieces of literature, art, and music have been rejected by so-called authorities. Many people who have become great were at one time considered by others as inferior. Even Jesus was accused of working with the devil.

There are several good reasons why we should not judge: (1) we do not know the circumstances or the situation; (2) we are never completely impartial; we are always prejudiced to some extent; (3) we have the tendency to bring others down so that we can make ourselves look better; (4) we judge others in order to cover up our own faults; (5) our shortcomings are often much worse than the other person's failures; (6) only God is good enough to judge people by his own standard.

If we see how bad our own faults are, we will not be very anxious to point out the faults of others. Judge your own selves harshly; be easy on others.

The gospel (Good News) is to be presented to everyone. However, we must face the reality that there are some who will not accept the word of God. There are some who have turned against God so completely that they will never accept Jesus Christ or anything concerning religion. Dogs have no understanding of right and wrong. Many people have also lost this ability to know good from bad. Pigs will not appreciate valuable jewelry. They do not understand values. There are many people who have lost their sense of values. There are some who seem unfit for Christianity; they simply will not listen. Leave these people to God.

What Kind of God
Matthew 7:7-11

What kind of God do we talk to when we pray? Jesus reveals that God will give us gifts greater than any our human fathers can give us. But we must ask and sometimes we must keep asking. We are assured that God will answer our prayers in his own wisdom. He will not give us less than we need: a stone when we ask for bread, or a serpent if we ask for a fish. Both of these items were food necessary for life. A stone resembled a loaf of bread. When Jesus was tempted for forty days, the stones reminded him of bread. A serpent lived in the water but could not be eaten. Jewish law said only that which has scales and fins may be eaten.

A Positive Rule
Matthew 7:12

Jesus was not really saying anything new. This is known as the "Golden Rule." Our Lord was not the first person to express it, but he was the first to make it a positive rule. Confucius said, "What you do not want done to yourself, do not do to others." Christianity is doing good to others, not refraining from doing anything. It is easy not to do anything, but we are responsible for others, and as Christians we should do for others as we would want them to do for us. If we base our lives on not doing, we have a useless religion.

Actions Must Agree With Words
Matthew 7:13-28

Entering the kingdom of God, that is, being faithful to God and what he wills for us (wants us to do), is not easy.

The Christian life demands making a choice: obeying God through Jesus Christ or following our own desires. If we go through life without submitting our lives to God, then we will destroy ourselves because we have broken the relationship between ourselves and God. "Destruction" means "separation from God."

Neither can we enter through the gate and follow the way if we do good works and deeds only to let others see how good we are, or to draw attention to ourselves.

In the early church, there were prophets who traveled from church to church speaking messages they believed came from God. (A prophet is one who has been given the spirit of God and is called by God.) There were certain tests made to determine if they were true prophets. *The Didache,* written around A.D. 100, gives regulations on the prophets. A true prophet was to be honored and respected. There were tests to determine if a prophet was authentic: If he stayed more than two days as a guest, he was a false prophet; if he asked for money in addition to bread, he was false; if he didn't practice what he preached, he was untrue; if he asked to have a meal set before him while he was speaking in the Spirit, he was false; if he was not willing to work for his food, he was to be ignored as a prophet.

One of the marks of a false prophet today is the taking of credit for what has been done instead of giving the credit to God. Is a person doing religious work to enhance his or her own image and to make himself or herself famous? Outwardly he or she appears to be doing God's work; inwardly he or she may only want personal prestige and gain.

We can identify a false prophet by what he or she produces. Some of these evil products might be: division among Christians; indifference to God's word; the idea that I am right and others are wrong; the belief that only my church or denomination is doing God's will and others are not.

Jesus is saying that a person may outwardly do everything that religion calls for. One may be able to preach great sermons, teach fine Sunday school lessons, give help to the poor, do great things in the name of Christianity, or even bring non-believers to conversion, but if it is done out of the wrong motive then a person has condemned himself. God knows what is in a person's heart and mind.

Jesus himself will be the one who judges us. Eventually all of the people of the world will have to face Jesus Christ on the day of judgment. God has given the responsibility of judging all men and women to his Son.

The Parable of the Two Houses is addressed to those who have heard what Jesus has to say. It demands a decision from the hearers. Those who choose to accept his words and build their lives on them are like a man who builds a house on a firm foundation. No problem or disaster or loss or any amount of suffering will be able to tear a person apart mentally or physically or spiritually. Those who reject the teachings of Jesus invite disaster to their lives. With these words of warning the Sermon on the Mount ends.

The Worst of Diseases

Matthew 8:1-4

Chapters five, six and seven have given us the words of Jesus, now chapter eight tells of his deeds which, of course, are miracles.

Today, if we have a disease, we are placed under the protection of a hospital. In Jesus' time a person with leprosy was forced to live outside any town surrounded by a wall. He was not allowed to put his head into any house. It was against the Law to greet a leper, and no one was allowed to get closer than six feet away from one. People with leprosy were forced to stay away from everyone except other lepers. The disease itself was horrible. It caused decay of skin, mental disorders, loss of feeling, and eventual death. If a person with this disease lived a long time, a hand or a foot might drop off. All Jews were forbidden to come in contact with one who had this dreaded disease.

Here, the leper and Jesus both broke Jewish laws. The leper threw himself in front of Jesus; this was closer than the Law allowed. Jesus held out his hand and touched him, also forbidden. The leper saw in Jesus the power to remove his disease; his faith made him well. We see that Jesus disregarded a law which made human need less important than sanitary conditions.

On the other hand, Jesus showed his respect for another section of the Law which required that one who is cured must go to a priest to be certified that he or she is healed. In Leviticus 14, there is the rite of purification in the unlikely event that someone was cured of leprosy.

Jesus did not want the account of his miracles broadcast all over the country. Palestine was filled with men who were looking for a military leader, a Messiah. It was also a country which had witnessed many uprisings and revolts. Many leaders had arisen, only to be stopped or wiped out by the great power of Rome. Jesus did not want to be thought of as a commander of a force to overthrow the Roman government. He wanted to change persons' hearts so that they would see the power of love, not the power of physical force.

No Greater Faith
Matthew 8:5-13

It is amazing that Roman centurions possessed abilities to perceive who Jesus was better than most of his disciples. The first Gentile convert was a centurion named Cornelius. He was the first non-Jew to accept the Christian faith. Two centurions helped Paul, and another one made an observation while Jesus hung on the cross that he was the son of God.

There are several things which stand out in this story: (1) The centurion, who could not have known too much about Jesus, came to him knowing that he had the power to heal. (2) The centurion loved his servant enough to want him healed. Slaves in that time were considered human tools, not people, so it was unusual for a master to be so concerned about the life of a slave. (3) The centurion was humble and did not consider himself worthy enough for Jesus to come into his house. (4) The centurion believed that Jesus did not have to be physically present in order to heal the servant. The centurion perceived that since he was in command of other soldiers (human forces), and they obeyed him; and that Jesus was in command of spiritual forces, then they would obey him. This is faith at its peak. The servant was healed.

Jesus issued a warning that members of his own nation

might be excluded from God's kingdom because of their refusal to believe in him. It also applies to those who are born and raised under the influence of the church who have not obeyed God. They may find themselves excluded also.

Peter's Mother-in-law
Matthew 8:14-17

Jesus' headquarters were in Capernaum at Peter's house. When Jesus returned there, he found Peter's mother-in-law sick with a fever. Malaria was common in that area, so she might have had this illness. Unlike other healings, no crowd was around to watch; it was done quietly with a few witnesses at the most.

As soon as she was healed she did not go out and tell all her neighbors about this miracle, she instead returned to her tasks of housework and of making Jesus comfortable on his return from his travels. She used the gift of God to help others. This is the way all of us should try to live. We should use the gifts that God has given us to their fullest.

After all the work that Jesus had done that day, he deserved a rest. People were meant to work during the day and rest in the evening. This was not the case with Jesus. Even in the evening we find him helping others. Human needs are more important than rest for ourselves. We discover when we serve others the strength will come. Here, Matthew uses another quotation from the Old Testament.

Following Jesus Is Not Easy
Matthew 8:18-22

Not all the scribes and Pharisees were opposed to Jesus. John's Gospel tells us that Nicodemus was a Pharisee and he admired Jesus. This man was so convinced that Jesus was a great leader and teacher, that he made a pledge that he would go with Jesus wherever he went. The Pharisees were familiar with the Jewish laws. There were 613 separate laws: 365 were negative and 248 were positive. There were more things you were not supposed to do than there were things you were to do. Some of these laws were unnecessary and some were ridiculous. Jesus ignored many of the laws which put ceremony above human needs. Jesus healed on the Sabbath; this was against the law. He ate grain from the fields on the Sabbath, also against the law. It is amazing that any Pharisee would want to follow Jesus, but this one did. And when he said he would follow Jesus, Jesus told him to think seriously about what he was really saying. Jesus would be traveling around Galilee and Judea, often eating and sleeping under the stars. So would his disciples. They would have no steady income like the Pharisee was used to getting. The comforts of home would be gone; the security of a job would end. Those who respected the Pharisee would turn against him. His whole life would be completely changed if he followed Christ. Jesus said to him, "Be sure of what you are doing before you follow me. You must count the cost."

Another man who was already a disciple said, "Let me go and bury my father, and then I will follow you." Jesus gave the impression that paying last respects to a dead father was unimportant. In the time of Jesus the funeral of a father was so important that the children were excused from several obligations. It was also a sacred duty to give a father a good burial. Why would Jesus be so cold? One explanation puts this in a different light. "To bury a father" meant that a son had certain duties and responsibilities to his family. As long as his father was alive he could not leave home. What he was saying to Jesus was that he wanted to put off following Jesus until sometime in the future when he had supposedly fulfilled all his obligations. Jesus said that if we are going to follow his way, we cannot put it off. Also, God's work takes precedence over the family duties.

Stopping the Storm
Matthew 8:23-27

The Sea of Galilee is not really a sea, it is more like a lake; it is only thirteen miles from north to south and no more than eight miles east to west. The geographical location of the lake makes it possible for sudden storms to come up. It can be very peaceful on the water, and then all of a sudden, winds are blowing and waves are springing up, tossing around any boat that happens to be in the water.

In this passage the disciples began to panic, and Jesus remained asleep. They woke him up because they were afraid of drowning, and Jesus stopped the storm. The important thing about this event is not so much that Jesus stopped the storm but that he can give us calm in the midst of storms in our lives. When we bring the presence of Jesus Christ into our lives, our problems and difficulties can be faced in a calm way. Just as Jesus had power over a natural occurrence in nature, he has power over the storms of our lives.

Demons Are Driven Out
Matthew 8:28-34

In Jesus' time people believed that sickness and mental illness were causes by demons. It was estimated that over seven million were in existence. One of the easiest ways, it was believed, for a demon to enter a person was by getting on his food when he ate. If a person was to be cured, he was going to have to be convinced that the demon had really left him. The area around tombs was supposed to be a favorite place for demons to live.

These two men were so wild that people were afraid to come near the place. And even Jesus was taking a risk getting close to them. It was believed that when the Messiah came, he would defeat all demons. That is why they asked him if he had come to torture them before the proper time. In order to be cured they had to have some visible proof that the demons had left. And so the herd of pigs provided the evidence that could be seen. The demons left the men, went into the pigs, and then caused the pigs to run down the bank into the water and drown. It was also believed that water was fatal to demons. This story also says that a person's mental and physical well-being is more important than a herd of animals. The people probably wanted Jesus to leave the area because they were afraid of his great powers.

The Paralyzed Man
Matthew 9:1-8

Capernaum had become Jesus' home in the early part of his ministry. While he was there some people brought a man, who was unable to move, to Jesus for healing. It was not the faith of the sick man which brought about his healing, but rather it was the faith of his friends. Where faith is present Jesus can heal, even if it is not the faith of the person to be cured. It was believed that sickness was the result of some sin. Often it was the result of some wrong doing, but we have long since learned that this is not always so. In order for a person to have been healed, obviously his sins must be forgiven and their influence removed. But when Jesus forgave the man's sins, his critics accused him of claiming to be God, because they believed that only God could forgive sins. Jesus proved that he had been given the power to forgive, just as God does, by restoring this man to good health.

An Unusual Choice
Matthew 9:9

Tax collectors were hated by the Jewish people. They had to bid for their jobs or buy their positions. People did not always know how much taxes they were supposed to pay because communication was poor; there were no newspapers or radios. The tax collectors also worked for Rome, which did nothing to help their popularity, and they were only responsible for an agreed sum. Anything over and above this they could keep for themselves, making many very wealthy. When Jesus called Matthew, his disciples must have questioned his choice.

Only the Ill Need a Doctor
Matthew 9:10-13

Jesus associated with all kinds of people; he did not show favoritism toward any one class of people. The term "sinner" did not apply always to an immoral person. We remember that religion in the time of Jesus consisted of following hundreds of rules and regulations. Many people did not practice all or even a few of these religious rules. Since the religious people of that time believed that obeying God's will consisted of obeying the rules, then those who did not obey were considered sinners. Sinners were the ones who were not too careful about all the little "thou shalt nots." On the other hand many of these "sinners" felt that they did not measure up to God's standards. They knew they did not have the right relationship with God. They knew they were not righteous; they needed help. Jesus came to help those who realized they were not righteous or good enough on their own. The scribes and Pharisees believed that they were good in God's sight and needed no help. Those who are well (think they are well) have no need of a physician. Giving a helping hand to one who is in trouble or suffering is more important than going through the motions of appearing religious.

Fasting
Matthew 9:14-17

Fasting (going without food for a period of time) was a religious practice of the time. Giving to the poor and prayer were two other great works of religious life. Jesus was not saying that he and his disciples should not fast. But the time for fasting was inappropriate because he was with them. He compared his coming with a wedding. A wedding in those days was one of the happiest affairs of the times. Weddings would last for several days. It was a time of festivities, of eating, drinking, and having a good time. Jesus pictures himself as a bridegroom, and as long as he is with them they should be joyful. The time would come when he would be put to death and then they could fast. This is one of the first hints that he would be put to death.

Jesus had come with a new idea; his coming meant that the old ideas of a person's relationship to God must be replaced with Jesus Christ as the center. The new message that Jesus was bringing would not fit into the old religious forms. Faith in Jesus Christ himself would be the new form.

Four Healings
Matthew 9:18-34

The first one to come to Jesus was a ruler in a synagogue (Mark and Luke tell us). The rulers were generally opposed to what Jesus was doing, and it may seem strange that he would come to Jesus for help. It is also possible that he had tried many doctors and none of them could help his daughter, so he came to Jesus as a last resort. He came to Jesus out of desperation and not out of trust. Despite this the ruler's daughter was healed.

The woman who had been ill for twelve years approached Jesus, believing that if she could only touch his clothing she would be made well. This is superstition, like the touching of sacred objects, or the putting of hands on the radio or the television in order to be healed. Still Jesus healed her.

The two blind men wanted to be cured of their handicap. But they called Jesus "Son of David." Their idea of Jesus was that he was to be a great military leader like King David. Jesus rejected this conception of himself; he would not win the people by force but by love and concern. Even though they had the wrong idea of who Jesus was, still they were cured. Jesus is willing to help anyone who trusts in him even though that person might not understand who he is. Our faith is not in proportion to our intelligence. We can come to him just as we are. Knowing Christ is what matters, not how much we know about him.

Once again, Jesus healed a man who could not speak. But his enemies accused him of bringing about the expulsion of demons, which were believed to be the cause of all illness, by working along with the chief of all demons, Beelzebul (Satan). This same charge against Jesus appears later on in Matthew.

Everywhere that Jesus went there were people in need; they were ill, frustrated, and had little hope. Even with all of his powers, Jesus was not able to help all the people. He needed others who would work in his name. The same is true today.

Instructions to the Twelve Disciples
Matthew 10:1-42

Jesus appointed twelve disciples to go out to the people of

Israel, preaching and healing. He told them to travel light and live by the hospitality of the people with whom they came in contact. They were to bless the places that received them and move on from places where they were rejected.

They were to go out to the people of Israel first before they went to the Gentiles. Israel had been chosen by God to be faithful to him and to tell the people of other nations about the one true God. But the people of Israel often ignored God and were disobedient to him. Because they failed to be faithful, they could not accomplish the second task — that of revealing God and what he required to others.

So Jesus sent his workers out to the people in order to give them another chance to be faithful to God. Some would accept them and others would reject them. Shaking the dust off the feet was symbolic of rejection.

Sodom and Gomorrah were cities which had existed hundreds of years before. They were filled with all kinds of vice and corruption. The names of the cities were (and are) synonomous with "evil." The book of Genesis tells how God destroyed the cities because they had become so perverted and godless. But Jesus says that the judgment against these two cities would not be as severe as the judgment against the residents of those towns who rejected him and the message that he brought. The disciples were to go to the towns and villages of Palestine. A community which would have nothing to do with the Gospel was inviting disaster upon itself.

Many of the sins of Sodom and Gomorrah were committed out of ignorance, but the people of Jesus' time had no excuse because they had heard what God required of them from the mouths of the disciples. They had the opportunity to accept or reject God's offer. And if they rejected it, judgment would be far worse.

Several years after Jesus' death, Christians were persecuted severely by the Romans and the Jews. They suffered if they claimed to believe in Christ. Matthew wrote his Gospel when persecutions were common. He tells us that Jesus assured his disciples that they would not have to worry about what they were to say when they were arrested or delivered up to authorities. God would give them the words to say in their defense.

It would be hard being a Christian. It might mean separation from families. It might mean that close relatives would turn against others in the family because they had chosen to follow Christ.

Jesus said that his followers should avoid becoming martyrs if possible. If they were rejected in one place, they were to get out of there and go to another place where they might be able to do some good. The conversion of Israel would take a long time. Even today, most of the Jewish people do not accept Jesus Christ as the Son of God, the Messiah.

Jesus would be persecuted and finally killed. His disciples would not be any better off; they must expect a rough road, too. Jesus had been accused of working with the devil; so, too, his followers would suffer the same fate.

Do not worry about what you do or say if you follow Jesus. People will not always accept what God wants them to hear. There will be opposition, even the possibility of death. But do not fear what other men can do to you, because God knows you and everything you are doing; he is always with you to give you strength.

Being committed to Jesus Christ means a person must make it known by what he says and what he does. One cannot be a Christian in secret.

We may wonder how Jesus could say that he had "not come to bring peace, but a sword," after the Sermon on the Mount. But here the meaning has to do with the struggle of the Christian. Following Christ will not be a bed of roses. It will be more like warfare. The soldier may be called upon to give up possessions, family and even his life for the sake of Christ. If we live only for ourselves, our lives become worthless, but if we live for someone else or for a higher good, then we find the true meaning of life.

If we honor a servant of Jesus Christ we are honoring him. The "little ones" are the less important followers of the Lord.

The Question of John the Baptist
Matthew 11:1-9

Jewish people believed that the Messiah would come and defeat the nation which controlled them. In Jesus' time it was

Rome. Before that time, the nation of Israel had been dominated by several other major powers on earth: Assyrians, Babylonians, Persians, Egyptians, and Syrians. Also, Alexander the Great had conquered the known world and had forced the Greek culture on the nations he controlled. The people of Palestine had been dominated by others for over seven hundred years. They were looking for a military leader like King David who would lead them to victory. Jesus was not acting like a commander of any army, so John the Baptist wondered if he was really the Messiah who was to come.

John the Baptist had been put into prison for criticizing Herod Antipas. Herod had taken his brother's wife for himself and had gotten rid of his own wife. John the Baptist let Herod know that he had done wrong. It was a dangerous thing to criticize anyone who was in power, so John was put into a prison.

When John's disciples came to Jesus to ask if he were the Messiah, Jesus replied by pointing out that blind people could see, crippled people could walk, the deaf would hear, diseases were cured, and people were discovering the true meaning of God's word. These were the signs that the prophets had foretold. Most important was the fact that the people were hearing the good news of Jesus Christ.

The Jews believed that before the Messiah could come, Elijah the prophet would return. John is the Elijah who was spoken of by the prophet Malachi (verse 4:5).

The Messiah had come and many people did not recognize him. Jesus himself was the Messiah.

Jesus talked to the people about his cousin John the Baptist. He asked them if they had gone out in the desert to see an ordinary man. (A "shaken reed" was an expression for a common sight). Or did they go out to see a man of wealth and ease? Or did they think that he was merely a prophet, one who spoke what God wanted people to hear. John was more than this, he was the forerunner of the Messiah, he was the Elijah.

Why would Jesus say that John was not as great as the least in the kingdom of heaven? It is because John would be executed before he would know about the New Covenant of Jesus Christ. Jesus Christ marked a new beginning, a new understanding of God. John was the last of the Old Covenant prophets. John was tough and threatening; Jesus was kind and gentle.

John did not live long enough to understand what Jesus was doing. He did not have the advantage others would have who lived during and after the time of Jesus.

Jesus compared the people to children who did not want to dance when the time was right for dancing, nor did they mourn when it was fitting to mourn. They would always find fault with whatever was offered. John lived a life of abstinence; he had no money, no luxuries, no fancy clothes. He did not waste anything, and he did not indulge in pleasures. He did not eat or drink anything more than was necessary for life. So he was accused of being crazy.

Jesus, on the other hand, ate and drank with sinners, went to parties, had a good time, and did it with all kinds of people, sharing their joys. He was accused of living a wild life, with evil people. (When people do not want to hear the truth, they can always find something to criticize.)

Jesus Can Judge and Bless
Matthew 11:20-29

Here is a clue that there is much that Jesus did that we know nothing about. The Gospels tell us nothing concerning the events in these cities which are mentioned. John's Gospel states that "if everything had been written down about Jesus and what he did, the world would not contain enough books that could be written." The people in these towns had seen the power of God through Jesus himself, yet they would not believe in him. Those in Tyre and Sidon did not have the opportunity, so judgment would not be as severe. Years before, the city of Sodom had been destroyed because of its corruption. Jesus was saying that if the residents of that place had witnessed the works of Jesus they would have repented. Jesus lived in Capernaum, yet they rejected his message.

Jesus was not speaking against intellectuals, nor was he saying that ignorance was to be preferred to knowledge. The "wise and understanding" were the scribes who were filled with the knowledge of the Law and Scriptures, yet they were ignorant of the true knowledge of God. "Knowledge" in the Bible does not mean knowing facts about someone, but rather indicates a relationship between two people. God knows us as we really are. Are we trying to know God? It does not matter how high our "IQ" might be, or how much knowledge of subjects we have accumulated. Religion consists of having a close personal relationship with our Maker and the Revealer of God, Jesus Christ.

Jesus was stating his authority as the Son of God. He has the same power as God the Father; he is judge of the world. To him we will all give an account of our lives. We can only know God through Jesus Christ.

As we have said before, the religion of the Jews was concerned with obeying all sorts of laws. There were 613 commandments, 365 negative and 248 positive. These had become a burden to people. They were difficult to remember, much less to obey. Those who did not obey every letter of the Law were made to feel as though God was going to condemn them for failure to live up to every detail. It had become a burden.

Jesus disregarded many of these laws, as we shall see in the next chapter. People were more important. He says, "Come to me, and I will give you rest," i.e., rest from the worry of trying to obey senseless rules and regulations. Jesus does not require us to carry a yoke that is more than we are able to bear. (A yoke was used on oxen for pulling equipment to plow fields and other work. The yokes were made to fit each ox individually.) The burdens he asks us to carry are suited for us; they are given to us according to our ability to bear them.

Needs Before Ritual
Matthew 12:1-8

The Jewish Law said that pulling corn off the plants was wrong on the Sabbath day. It was permitted during any other day of the week. If a person or persons were traveling through the country and became hungry, it was considered right to walk into a corn field and help one's self to the corn. The disciples were not accused of stealing, they were accused of working on the Sabbath. Any kind of harvesting was considered work, and if one pulled the corn off the stalk, it was work according to the Law. A

Jew was not permitted to cook or even start a fire on that day. He was not allowed to lift anything that weighed more than the weight of two dried figs. The offense of the disciples was doing on the Sabbath what the Law forbade.

Jesus reminded his critics of the time David went into the tabernacle (the Temple had not been built), and he and his men helped themselves to the bread that was used in the ritual sacrifice to God. They were not condemned for satisfying their hunger. Human needs are more important than proper ritual. Jesus also let them know that their own priests broke the Law every week. They started fires, they moved things which weighed over the weight of two dried figs. They did work which was forbidden by the Law if there was to be a Temple service. No one objected to this so why should the Pharisees complain about Jesus' disciples? People are much more valuable than the stones of a temple or any building. God wants his people to show mercy and compassion to each other, rather than allow a law or any regulation to prevent them from helping others.

The New Testament was written in capital letters in the Greek language. When it was translated, we do not know if "son" referred to Jesus himself or to any man. An ordinary man was often referred to as a "son of man." If this were the meaning, then Jesus was saying that the Sabbath belonged to any person: "the Sabbath was made for man." If he was referring to himself, then Jesus could permit his disciples to take care of their needs, because he was the master of the Sabbath.

Here again, the Law was involved in the healing of a man with a withered hand. The Law did not permit a person's condition to be improved on the Sabbath, but steps could be taken to prevent an ailment from becoming worse. A bandage could be changed on that day, but no medication could be applied to help the healing process. Only a life and death situation could be taken care of on the Sabbath. And since a withered hand was not going to affect the span of life, it was against the law to heal it on that day. He could wait until the next day according to the Law. But the Law also said that it was all right to help animals on the Sabbath; are not people more valuable than sheep? Doing good on the Lord's day should take precedence over regulations that prevent doing good. This only served to make the Pharisees angrier than ever, and they left the synagogue thinking of ways to get him out of the way.

Jesus did not try to become a martyr. He avoided trouble whenever possible.

Jesus healed many people, and always requested that they keep it to themselves. Why did he want these healings kept quiet? It was because of the people of Palestine. They had been ruled by foreign nations for years, and they were looking for freedom from domination. They were also looking for a Messiah, a military leader like King David, to help them overthrow the Romans. Riots had been common, rebellion was in the air. Jesus did not want anyone to think of him as being a potential military commander. Jesus' way was the way of love, not of force. If the word had gotten around that he might lead them in an attempt to gain their independence from Rome, it would mean much unnecessary bloodshed.

Jesus' purpose was to overcome the forces of evil by his own method, not by violence. True freedom comes only when we give our lives to Jesus Christ and let him lead us. Jesus' kingdom rules us from within ourselves.

The quotation from Isaiah was originally applied to Cyrus the Great, ruler of Persia, who allowed the Jewish exiles to return to Palestine.

Calling Good, Evil
Matthew 12:22-32

Jesus healed another man who had suffered from loss of eyesight and also loss of speech. People believed he was possessed by a demon, so in order to be healed, the man had to be convinced that the demon had left him. The people saw this great miracle and some concluded that Jesus might be the Messiah. "Son of David" means that they regarded him as a leader similar to King David, who had united the twelve tribes of Israel, making them a strong military force.

When the Pharisees overheard these comments their reaction was to accuse Jesus of working with the devil, Beelzebul, the chief of demons.

But this accusation would make no sense. The main purpose of demons, it was believed, was to bring evil, havoc, and misery to people. Why would Satan want to work against his own forces? He would be divided against himself, contributing to his own defeat.

There were many Jewish healers and exorcists in Jesus' day. In their healing of others they prescribed an elaborate set of measures a person must follow in order to be healed. It was similar to some of the practices used in witchcraft throughout history. If they believed that others exorcised demons by God's power, then they could call what Jesus was doing evil.

The strong man was Satan. Jesus was saying that He must first subdue him before He can eject his forces from the lives of individuals.

No one can become a Christian and remain neutral. A Christian must do all he or she can to oppose the forces of evil at work in the world. Sitting on the fence and doing nothing is one way of helping the enemy. If we do not follow and support Jesus, we are opposing him, often without realizing it.

The sin against the Spirit has been a source of many questions. There are some who fear that they have committed a sin against the Holy Spirit and will never be forgiven; this worry has caused much unnecessary grief. The mere worry about committing the unforgivable sin is proof that the sin was never committed.

Jesus made this statement immediately after being accused of working in partnership with evil. Those who accused him were labeling something which was beneficial to a man as being bad. They called "good" which was done the opposite of what it was. They were calling it "evil."

The unforgivable sin is this very thing: it is the inability to distinguish right from wrong, good from bad, and moral from immoral. It is unforgivable because there is no repentance. A sin can only be forgiven if a person is sorry for his sin and pledges that he will not repeat it. If he does not know right from wrong, or believes that anything goes, he cannot repent; therefore there is no forgiveness.

This statement was made before the day of Pentecost, when the Holy Spirit was given to the disciples. The Jews understood less about the Holy Spirit than the later Christians did. The Spirit revealed God's truth and helped men and women understand it. The Spirit was God at work in the lives of people. To ascribe

God's work to the devil is the loss of spiritual perception.

Jesus Offends
Matthew 12:33-42

We will not be judged by the things we say which have been thought out beforehand. Many times we say words merely to impress others or exalt ourselves or make ourselves look good. Often we speak nice words, but down deep we would rather speak harsh words.

We will be judged by the words we have spoken which come out of our hearts and mouths when we have not prepared them. They are the things spoken when our guard is down, when we express our true feelings, our real thoughts. If we are suspicious, it will eventually show in our speech. If we hold hatred for another person within ourselves, it will make itself known by a careless word sooner or later. We cannot continue to pretend, because words from our mouths will reveal us in time. Only a change in our hearts will change our words.

Some of the religious leaders wanted to see Jesus perform a miracle to prove that God had sent him. They wanted a sign so that they would be satisfied that he was who he claimed to be. But Jesus refused by saying that this was an attitude of evil and unbelief. Jesus used the word "adulterous" to describe them. It does not mean that they were guilty of unfaithfulness to their wives. In the Old Testament, Israel is often described as being unfaithful to God, and the image is used in the comparison of God's chosen nation to an unfaithful wife. Hosea, the prophet, used this image to describe the Israel of his day. Adultery means "misplaced affections." The religious leaders had turned away from devotion to God to devotion to the Law.

The Gospel writer, Luke, does not mention that Jonah was in the belly of a whale for three days and nights. There is a good reason why Luke does not make this comparison. Jesus was not in the tomb for three days and nights. Since he was buried on Friday and rose from the dead on Sunday this would have been impossible. We miss the meaning of what Jesus is saying if we direct our attention to this analogy. The sign that Jesus meant is that of Jonah and his message. The sign that was perceived by the people of Nineveh was God's word through the mouth of Jonah. They accepted it and changed their ways from nonbelief to obedience to God. Jesus was the sign from God and the people are not recognizing this. The residents of Nineveh perceived God's warning from Jonah. The Queen of Sheba recognized God's wisdom through Solomon. But Jesus is greater than Jonah or Solomon. They merely spoke on God's behalf, but in Jesus they are confronted by God himself.

Evil Comes Back

Matthew 12:43-45

This parable can apply to the people of Israel or to individuals. Those who regarded themselves as religious had swept their lives clean of all wrong doing, so they thought. They believed that they were completely good because they observed the Law of God. But these Jews, by observing the laws down to the last detail, were allowing prejudice, contempt, indifference, and scorn to come into their minds and hearts. They were self-righteous. Outwardly they appeared to be free of unclean spirits, but inwardly they had allowed many more evil spirits to come into their lives.

We can rid ourselves of a bad habit or practice. We can clean up our lives and put away nagging sins that threaten to destroy us. But when we give up a bad thing we cannot simply dispense with it. It must be replaced by something good. A man can stop gambling but he must find some good to fill up the time which was formerly spent in gambling. Otherwise he will soon be back to wagering his money.

The Family of Jesus

Matthew 12:46-50

Jesus was not being cruel or indifferent toward his family. And we are not told that Jesus refused to see them. We do know that Mary did not understand him, and his brothers did not believe in him. His own friends from Nazareth thought he was nothing more than a carpenter they had known for several years.

What Jesus was pointing out was that those who believed in him and his words, those who followed him, those who were faithful, and those who loved him were members of his family.

The Parable of the Seed

Matthew 13:1-9

At this point in his ministry Jesus was found teaching more and more out-of-doors. He was not as welcome in the synagogues as he once was.

Parables were used by other teachers before Jesus. Parables are short stories that point to a truth. People remember stories about concrete events better than ideas or philosophies. Since there were no newspapers or books, people had to depend on their memories. And so a parable could teach truths that could be retained in the minds of those who heard them.

The "Parable of the Seed" was directed to those who heard God's word. The ground represented different kinds of hearers.

The first type was the hard ground which was in between the narrow strips of plowed land. This hard ground was the path that passers-by walked on. This person was so hardened by all that was opposed to God, that his mind was completely shut to all that God said to him.

The second kind of person was represented by the ground which was so shallow that it was really only a thin covering over the rocky ground. The seed would grow roots, but they were not allowed to go very deep for nourishment because they would hit rock. Because there was no depth, the sun would scorch the plant. This person was happy and was filled with joy when he heard God's word, but soon afterward, when a problem or a trial or some trouble occured, the Word of God had disappeared from his life.

The third kind of hearer was the one who knew what God required; he had a grasp of the Gospel, but he involved himself with the concerns, the affairs, and the interests of the world. Because he was so tied up with everyday matters, his devotion to God got crowded out.

The fourth kind was the one who had an open mind to the good news. He did not let trouble or problems or doubts take away his trust in God. He knew when to get interested in the world and when he should forget the world. He gave his time to God and the doing of his will. He realized that the world belonged to God and so did he. When he heard God's word he transformed it into action in God's service.

Why Parables?
Matthew 13:10-17

This section is hard to understand. It sounds as though Jesus was saying that only his disciples could know the mysteries of the Kingdom of God while the crowds were excluded. If this were true then there is no chance for any of us to receive and understand God's word. Mark and Luke do not clarify the question any better. They give the impression that Jesus spoke in parables to prevent people from understanding. But Jesus did not come to hide the truth; he came to show what God is like, to reveal God's truth. To compound the problem, verses 34-35 say exactly the opposite: that parables are given to reveal things which have always been hidden.

The disciples were to be happy because they were hearing and seeing Jesus Christ who was revealing more fully than ever before God's will for all people. The revelation of God had been incomplete until Jesus Christ came. Godly men and God's prophets desired to witness the very things Jesus' disciples were hearing and seeing. Matthew 13:18-23 is the explanation of the parable in verses 3-9 by Jesus himself. All Christian life must go beyond the mere hearing of what God has to say. It must be translated into action.

Parable of the False Wheat
Matthew 13:24-30

Darnel (weeds or tares) were plants that resembled wheat in the early stages of growth. They looked so similar to the wheat that it would have been impossible to tell them apart. As they progressed, the difference became obvious, but the roots had become so intertwined that the darnel could not be pulled up without taking the wheat along with it.

The enemy is Satan, the power of evil in the world, who comes along and plants the bad seed in the midst of the good. The good and evil exist side by side and it is hard to tell them apart. We are not to judge; only God, through his Son, will be able to tell the wheat from the darnel — the faithful from the unfaithful — when the day of judgment comes. Only God can tell the difference between the good and the bad.

Several More Parables
Matthew 13:31-52

The mustard seed is not the smallest seed, nor is the plant that comes from it the largest tree. However, in the Middle East, the mustard seed is the symbol of smallness. The mustard plant is much larger in that part of the world, sometimes attaining a height of twelve feet. The Kingdom of God has a small beginning but in time it will grow and become large. The growth of the Christian church bears this out. Three centuries after Christ, one-tenth of the population of the Roman Empire was Christian. Out of one hundred million people, ten million called themselves "followers of Christ."

Leaven was a piece of fermented bread that was placed in the dough to make it rise. Leaven was also symbolic of evil, because by nature leaven is decayed dough. It signified corruption. But Jesus used it in another sense. Leaven also transforms the dough from being flat and dry to being soft and moist. The Kingdom of Heaven transforms lives from being dull and useless to being joyous and productive. The work of the leaven is unseen but the results are clearly seen.

Here the explanation of why Jesus spoke in parables makes more sense than does the explanation in verses 13-19. Parables were spoken to help people perceive the Kingdom rather than hide it from them.

The parable of the "Treasure in the Field" points out that the kingdom can be found by accident, while the "Pearl of Great Value" tells us that it can be found after a long search. In both cases the finder gives up all former possessions in order to gain the Kingdom.

The "Parable of the Net" is another way of stating the "Parable of the Wheat and the Tares." The good and the bad exist together and will be separated at the Last Judgment.

In order to become a scribe, a man had to study for many years. Jesus may have used this term to describe "one who learns." A learner, who understands the meaning of the parables, can bring new truths out of old, familiar events.

Unwelcome in His Hometown
Matthew 13:53-58

Jesus returned to the place where he had lived as a child. The people of Nazareth had known him for years. They knew his parents and his brothers and sisters. The family was no different from any other family in that community. Jesus had been a carpenter like his father, Joseph. They were unimportant people, so the question arises, "Where did this man get all of his wisdom?" It certainly did not come from this small village.

Because of their unbelief Jesus could do little good there.

John the Baptist Is Murdered
Matthew 14:1-12

Herod suffered from a guilty conscience. He had stolen his brother's wife and married her. He had made a promise to his step-daughter Salome while he was drunk. He pledged to give her anything she wanted if she would only dance. She asked for the head of John the Baptist. Herod was afraid that John had come back from the dead in the form of Jesus.

More Miracles
Matthew 14:13-36

After hearing the sad news of the death of John the Baptist, Jesus tried to get away alone. He got into a boat to go to the other side of the lake, but the crowds went on foot around the water and met him on the opposite side. Jesus was so popular that the people did not lose interest in him after seeing and hearing him for several hours. They would not leave. He felt compassion for them; hunger would not cause them to return home.

We do not know the process involved in the converting of a few pieces of bread and fish into a great quantity. There have been explanations by those who do not accept the story literally.

One is that each person only ate a small fragment of bread and fish. This was the forerunner of the Sacrament of the Lord's Supper in which the small portion symbolizes the spiritual food of Jesus Christ.

Another says that the people knew that they would need food for the trip to see Jesus, and they had packed it away. They were selfish people, hiding their food so that they would not have to share it. Jesus merely brought about feelings of generosity among the people, causing them to share their bread and fish with others.

Most people probably accept the story of Jesus' multiplying the loaves and fish since it was in his power to do this. The point of the story is that Jesus provides for human needs even when it is not a life and death matter. None of the people would have starved or imperiled their health if they had not eaten that day.

The crowds left reluctantly while Jesus went up into the hills to be alone with God. He did this on many occasions, spending long hours in prayer.

Sometime between 3 and 6 a.m. Jesus approached the boat which was some distance out in the water. He was walking on the water. The disciples did not recognize him. After he identified himself, their fear was abated and it was Peter who wanted to duplicate this feat.

This story tells us that Jesus Christ is master even of the elements of the earth, the weather, the forces of nature. Second, it tells us that if we keep our attention and will focused on Jesus in faith we have the power and ability to do things which we cannot do alone. If doubt overtakes faith then we begin to flounder, and we lose the strength to do what only the power of God can provide. The lesson that Peter learned here no doubt helped him later on, just as our failures teach us we cannot depend solely on ourselves. The disciples realized that Jesus was no ordinary man.

Again, Jesus cured people of their diseases wherever he went.

Laws That Oppose Love
Matthew 15:1-9

The traditions and laws that were manufactured by the scribes down through the years often contradicted the commandments of God. One could declare his goods and property as being dedicated to God. The term for this was "Corban," which meant that a person did not have to use his possessions to help his parents when they were in need. This vow freed him from family obligations but did not deprive him from using his goods for his own benefit. This loophole allowed him to violate the fifth commandment. Washing hands in a certain way was only a ritual which had little value in serving God. It was only a human regulation which made no difference to God whether it was observed or not. Jesus accused the scribes and Pharisees of distorted priorities — they were concerned with trivialities and ignored the well-being of others.

Clean and Unclean
Matthew 15:10-20

What the religious leaders considered clean and unclean was only remotely connected with what was healthy and unhealthy. It was a ceremonial matter, not a matter of hygiene. To be clean meant that a person could approach and worship God. To be unclean meant he was unfit to do this.

The law stated what a person could and could not eat. Leviticus 11 lists all the foods on either list, those allowed and those forbidden. The only animals that could be eaten were ones with a cloven hoof and which chewed the cud. Cattle were acceptable, pigs were not because they didn't chew the cud.

Jesus stated that what a person ate did not determine his/her relationship to God. What matters is that which comes out of a person's mouth as the product of good or evil thoughts. It is the evil in the heart that cuts off true worship of God.

The scribes had even worked out an elaborate system of hand

washings to remove the uncleanliness that might have been incurred. The truly religious were expected to practice the washings before meals according to the regulations. Jesus was not condemning washing hands before meals, only the ceremony attached to it.

Jesus Leaves Palestine
Matthew 15:21-28

Jesus left his native country to be alone, to escape the crowds. He was getting close to the cross and he needed solitude to pray and contemplate his mission. This is the only time he left Palestine in his three years in the public. Even here he was recognized by a Canaanite woman. The Canaanites were ancient enemies of the Jews for hundreds of years.

She appealed to him to heal her daughter, but Jesus seemed to ignore her. Matthew places emphasis on the mission of Jesus to his own people. This is similar to the commissioning of the Twelve who go only among the citizens of Israel.

But this reply did not stop the woman from begging him for help. This time Jesus replied with a statement which sounds rude, "It is not fair to take the children's food and throw it to the pet dogs." Since we do not know the tone of voice Jesus used when he made this comment, we cannot be sure what he might have meant. The Jews sometimes referred to Gentiles as "dogs," which was not a term of endearment.

It is possible that the woman did not take offense at this because of the way in which it was said. It might mean, "It is not fair to give to the Gentiles what is meant to be given to the people of Israel."

Jesus was testing the woman's faith. She did not give up and replied with a witty remark, "Even the dogs can receive what was intended for the children because there is more than enough."

Jesus was impressed by her faith and healed her daughter.

More Cures and Another Miracle
Matthew 15:29-39

This is not a retelling of the event described before where over five thousand people were fed. In the first story there is grass where they are sitting; this story takes place in the desert. The crowds had been there for a longer time. It also took place in an area where there were many Gentiles ("they praised the God of Israel"). God's concern was (and is) extended not only to Israel but to all people.

They Again Request a Sign
Matthew 16:1-4

This time the Sadducees joined the Pharisees. Traditionally, they were enemies, the Pharisees holding to the tradition of the elders which was the oral and scribal law; the Sadducees rejected the tradition completely and accepted only the words of the first five books of the Bible (the Pentateuch). The Pharisees believed in the resurrection of the dead and angels while the latter did not. The Sadducees were members of the priestly sect and were also wealthy aristocrats.

Jesus pointed out that they could tell what the weather was going to be but they could not see the Kingdom of God coming in Jesus himself. The Pharisees looked for a Messiah while the Sadducees did not.

The sign of Jonah was Jonah and his message from God which had converted the Ninevites. Jesus and his message were the signs from God which the Pharisees and Sadducees were unable to see.

Beware of Yeast
Matthew 16:5-12

The hostility against Jesus was growing; the anxiety of the disciples over this may have caused them to forget about the provisions they would need. When Jesus said, "Beware of the leaven of the Pharisees," they thought he was talking about forgetting the bread. They had to buy bread and possibly they thought that Jesus was warning them about purchasing the wrong kind of bread. Jesus reminded them of the two miracles which had fed thousands of people. When Jesus was present they should not be worrying about trifles; they should put their trust in him.

The warning was against the "yeast of the Pharisees and the Sadducees." Yeast was symbolic of evil, because yeast spoiled dough. Yeast stood for all that was rotten and bad. Yeast spread through the dough and caused it to change. It symbolized the evil influence that corrupted life. The disciples understood that the teaching and beliefs of the Pharisees and Sadducees would corrupt the right understanding of God's relationship to men.

The Pharisees saw religion as a series of "dos" and "don'ts," of regulations and prohibitions. It was a legalistic religion which only looked at the outward acts and ignored the state of a man's heart.

The Sadducees saw life as a matter of wealth and political influence. Jesus warned against identifying God's favor with material goods and a person's position in the community. True religion comes from within, from loving God in a grateful, obedient attitude.

The Turning Point
Matthew 16:13-20

Once again Jesus withdrew to another territory outside the domain of Herod Antipas. This area was over twenty miles northeast of the Sea of Galilee. He had to have time to think about his mission. The days were getting short; he knew that the opposition was gaining momentum, and a plot was forming which would mean his eventual death.

Did anyone really understand who he was? Did anyone recognize him as God's Son? Would there be anyone to carry on his work after he was gone from earth? Would the Christian faith survive? He needed to know if his work could continue, so he asked the crucial questions: "Who do men say the Son of Man is?" And the second question was even more important, "Who do you say I am?"

There were some who believed that John the Baptist was such a great man that he had come back from the dead. Herod himself believed that Jesus might be John. Others believed him to be Elijah. This was a great compliment since Elijah was regarded as the greatest prophet. It was also believed that Elijah would return as the forerunner of the Messiah (Malachi 4:5).

They also thought that he might be Jeremiah, because this prophet had condemned the religious practices of his own day.

And then came the answer to the all-important question, "Who do you say I am?" It was Peter who gave the answer Jesus was looking for. "You are the Christ, the Son of the Living God." Peter confessed that Jesus was the long expected Messiah. "Messiah" means "annointed one." "Christ" is the Greek equivalent to "Messiah."

Peter came to this conclusion by means of faith. The perception of who Jesus really was came to him through the illumination and inspiration of God. No other person had convinced Peter of this; the recognition came from above. Recognizing Jesus as the Son of God comes only through faith, and faith is a gift from God.

Jesus gave him a new name, "Peter," which means "rock." "Cephas" is the name for "rock" in the Aramaic language. (Jesus and the disciples all spoke Aramaic).

What follows has been the source of many interpretations. The Roman Catholics believe that Peter was designated the first bishop or pope of the church. Protestants do not accept this interpretation.

What was meant by, "Upon this rock . . ."? There are several interpretations: The "rock" can refer to Jesus himself, or the "rock" is the truth that Jesus Christ is the Son of God. It can also mean that the "rock" is Peter's faith, or it may refer to Peter himself. These are several possibilities which have not been settled.

However, we do know that Peter was a key leader in the Church (the word "church" appears only one other time in Matthew; it never appears in the other Gospels). Peter would be the first member of the Church because he was the first to confess faith in Jesus Christ, the first to grasp who Jesus really was.

Hades was believed to be the place of the dead. In the Old

Testament it was believed that all the dead existed in a semi-conscious state in this place (in Hebrew it is called "Sheol"). The function of the gates was to keep the dead inside. But Jesus would overcome death and the gates would not keep him in. Death would no longer claim those who believed in him either.

Peter was to be given the keys of the Kingdom, symbolizing that he was the first to open the door of faith that leads to eternal life. Those who believe in Jesus Christ will enter the Kingdom; those who reject him will find the door locked.

Because the Messiah was expected to be a military leader like some of the kings of Israel, Jesus told his followers to keep his identity a secret. After his death and Resurrection the people would understand that his role was different from their expectations.

Prediction of Death
Matthew 16:21-23

Now, at least Peter knew who Jesus was and now he could reveal what was going to happen to him. Jesus would be put to death. He had caused severe opposition by his teaching, his miracles and his claim that he was sent by God. He was a threat to Jewish leaders and their positions. He would be killed, but the good news is that he would be raised from the dead on the third day. Instead of appreciating this announcement the disciples became indignant. This was not supposed to happen to the Messiah, the Son of God. He was supposed to conquer men, not be subdued by them.

Peter, who was elated over having pleased his Lord by his affirmation of faith only a short time before, found this unacceptable. Surely there must be a mistake; Jesus must be wrong. Peter let Jesus know how he felt about his future. "Get thee behind me, Satan," was the sharp reply.

Peter's reason for believing that Jesus should not die is obvious. No one can bear to hear from a close friend that he must die soon. It is natural for a devoted friend to want to prevent a premature death. Jesus' way was the path God had chosen for him to take in order to save the world. It was the hard way; Peter desired the easier way for his Lord. Peter's voice was the voice of temptation which Jesus had heard after his baptism. Satan had tempted him in the desert. If Jesus was going to be obedient to God, there would be no easy way out to accomplish his mission.

Requirements for Following Christ
Matthew 16:24-28

Jesus does not make soft and easy demands on his followers. Being a disciple means giving up things that the world offers which appear attractive and desirable. It means giving up self concern and personal safety. It means living for Jesus Christ and doing what he wants us to do.

The question might be asked if the disciples could understand at this point the meaning of the expression, "take up his cross." The disciples had no knowledge of what this meant, since Jesus had not gone from Jerusalem to Golgotha carrying his cross. How could the disciples have known what method would be used to kill him?

By losing one's life in service to God, i.e., forgetting about ourselves, we find eternal life. If we live only for ourselves we will throw our lives away. We were created for the purpose of helping one another and loving God.

This saying also applied to the situation in the Roman Empire after the death of Jesus. Persecutions arose, forcing Christians to give up their allegiance to Jesus Christ and confess that the Caesar was God. Those who refused to do this were tortured or murdered. Many renounced their Christian faith in order to save their lives. But by saving their lives on earth, they ran the risk of losing eternal life. Those who refused to call the Roman emperor a god would lose their earthly lives but might gain eternal life for themselves. We must remember that judgment and eternal destiny are solely the decision of God.

Verse 27 pertains to the Last Judgment while verse 28 is about the destruction of Jerusalem which took place in A.D. 70.

The Transfiguration
Matthew 17:1-8

In this mysterious event, Moses and Elijah appeared on a mountain with Jesus. The event signifies the confirmation of Jesus as Son of God, having a definite mission. Moses represented the giving of the Law, while Elijah was the representation of prophecy. Jesus had come to fulfill the Law and the Prophets. This was a sight that the disciples did not want to see ended. Peter wanted to construct shelters for the three men. The voice from heaven was the reaffirmation that Jesus was God's Son who was to be the world's Savior. Jesus' destiny was now certain; the road was clearly mapped out. The experience on the mountain was the reassurance which Jesus needed. The presence of God means that all fear is banished in those who know they are unworthy. They know that God will show mercy to them.

What About Elijah?
Matthew 17:9-13

The prophet Malachi had prophesied that before the Messiah appeared, Elijah would precede him. But Jesus told the disciples that Elijah had already come and was not recognized. He was murdered in Herod's palace. The same fate will come to Jesus soon. Elijah had come as John the Baptist and the people had not realized it.

The Epileptic Boy
Matthew 17:14-21

The disciples were unable to heal the boy with epilepsy. Even though they had been given power over diseases, they could not bring about his cure. If Jesus was upset over their lack of faith, what must he think about the ineffectiveness of Christians today? Jesus keeps his promises; faith is the assurance that anything is possible with God.

The father did not give up after the failure of Jesus'

representatives. He went directly to the source, Jesus himself. He did not doubt his ability to heal his son.

"Removing mountains" was not a phrase to be taken literally by Jesus' contemporaries. It meant "to remove difficulties." Faith in Jesus Christ means that difficult problems can be solved which hinder our efforts. It means that we can cross barriers as if they were not there.

The Second Prophecy of the Passion
Matthew 17:22-23

Jesus stated again that he would be killed and afterwards be raised from the dead. Apparently, the disciples did not pay too much attention to this.

Jesus Pays Taxes
Matthew 17:24-27

The temple was supported by the taxes paid by every male Jew over the age of twenty. The amount was one-half shekel. Peter was asked if Jesus paid the tax and he assumed that Jesus did. If Jesus refused to pay the tax, his enemies would have grounds for an accusation.

Peter told Jesus about the question, and Jesus asked another one of him. "Who pays the tribute to a king, his sons or foreigners?" The answer was "foreigners." A king would not ask his own family to pay, so they were exempt. The Temple was God's house and Jesus was his Son. So by rights he should be exempt from the temple tax. But his critics would not accept his sonship, so in order to set a good example and not upset anyone, he paid the tax. The miracle is unimportant in the story.

The Greatest in the Kingdom
Matthew 18:1-4

Children have qualities and attitudes which are appropriate for all Christians. They know themselves to be of less importance than others, especially adults. They are not ambitious or self-seeking. They have an attitude of trust that their needs will be provided for. They have a sense of dependence on those who love them. They do not pretend to be greater than they really are; they are content to be themselves. Their belief in God is not based on reason or arguments; they believe without question. They know that if they are to live in the world they must be obedient to those who care for them. They have the ability to forgive and forget injuries done to them. They are not too concerned about what others think of them. They accept what they do not fully understand. They have the characteristics that should mark a Christian.

The Great Responsibility

Matthew 18:5-10

Children are impressionable. They learn from adults what is right and wrong. They learn habits, both bad and good, which will affect their later lives. They accept what they are taught, often without question. They are influenced by the words and actions of elders.

Jesus stressed the awesome responsibility that parents and all adults should have in training children to become mature people. It is bad enough to sin against God in our own lives, but to cause someone else to go wrong is many times worse.

There are countless temptations in the world. They are not easy to overcome once a person gives in to them. All temptations should be eliminated from our lives. We should never cause someone else to be tempted, nor should we bring another person into a situation where temptation can come.

We should see in every child the possibilities which can develop, doing all we can to see that the potential is realized. Everything depends on how a child is trained and treated by others.

A Sheep Gets Lost
Matthew 18:12-14

A shepherd will devote himself completely to the recovery of one lost sheep, even if it is only a little one. We should give of ourselves in order to guide a small child in the right direction. Each individual is important.

Settling Disputes
Matthew 18:15-18

It is questionable whether Jesus could have said this. The advice sounds more like the legalism of a church committee. Matthew wrote his Gospel after the church was already organized, and it could have been said by an ecclesiastical (church) leader. Jesus taught us to forgive others for the wrongs they do to us. He did not say that we should take strong measures against a person who will not admit his/her fault. We are to forgive regardless of the attitude of another person towards us.

Jesus could not have told his disciples to take it to the church for settlement; the church did not yet exist. This saying contradicts Jesus' attitude towards tax-collectors and non-Jews.

Praying Together
Matthew 18:19-20

This is a saying that can lead to disappointment if taken literally. We know that we could not have anything we wanted even if several people agreed on what it was. On the other hand, when we pray, we have the assurance that Jesus is present with us.

In Bible times a person's name was an expression of the reality of that person. A name was descriptive of who he was. The name "Jesus" means "God is Salvation." To pray in his name means that we are calling on him to be with us as we meet with him. When Jesus is present in our prayer life, he enables us to ask for what is necessary and teaches us what we should pray for.

What is best for us will be granted to us by God.

How Much Forgiveness?
Matthew 18:21-22

The teachers of religion said that it was only necessary to forgive another person three times. The book of Amos stated that God forgave certain nations three times but not four. It was decided that humans were not more spiritual than God, so a person should not be required to do more than God. Peter went as far as to ask if he should forgive as many as seven times, four more than the requirement. Jesus answered by saying that a person must forgive always. There must never be a time when forgiveness is withheld.

Parable of the Debtor
Matthew 18:23-25

Jesus told a parable of a servant who owed ten million dollars. This was more than the annual income of the nation of Israel many times over. The servant could not pay and he begged for more time to repay. The master was so moved with compassion that he told him that the debt was canceled.

The servant went out and met another servant who owed him less than twenty dollars and demanded payment. He had him thrown in jail when he refused to pay. The report was given to the man who had forgiven the large debt and it angered him. So he had that servant thrown in jail for his lack of mercy.

The debt we owe to God is so great that we cannot ever pay it back. We have all failed to do what is right many times. We have forgotten God; we have sinned against him; we have neglected his will; and we have hurt others. Yet God can forgive us if we repent (turn to him and confess our sins).

Since God forgives the great debt we owe him, we must forgive others for the harm they have done to us. What others do to us is insignificant compared to what we have done to God.

Marriage and Divorce
Matthew 19:1-12

Marriage was not taken lightly in Palestine. Most men were expected to be married by the age of twenty. But there were some problems. Women were regarded as property; they had no rights. Marriages were usually arranged by the parents and it was possible to marry someone who had never been seen before by a marriage partner. In matters of divorce only the man could take steps to have the marriage dissolved. A woman could be divorced without her consent, but the man only by his consent. Grounds for divorce were sometimes minimal. A divorce could result if the wife ruined dinner, or talked to men in the streets, or if the husband found someone he liked better. Not everyone agreed with these grounds for divorce, but many did.

The Pharisees claimed that Moses had given rules for divorce. Jesus replied that they were allowed because the people were stubborn. A better standard is the one given by God that when two unite in marriage they become one body. They should never be separated.

Some can go through life remaining single while others should be married.

Jesus' Attitude Toward Children
Matthew 19:13-15

The disciples regarded children as intruders. But Jesus welcomed them and restated what he said before, that children have the characteristics that all Christians should possess.

The Wealthy Young Man
Matthew 19:16-22

A young man who had many riches came to Jesus asking what good deed he could do to inherit eternal life. Jesus asked him why he wanted to know about what was good. The problem with the rich man was that he thought he could gain eternal life by doing a good deed. He was just like the Pharisees who believed they could please God by their actions, by keeping the rules and regulations.

Jesus said that he could have eternal life if he kept the commandments. The ones he cited were the five of the Ten Commandments, those which deal with one's relationship to another person, and also the second part of the "great commandment."

The rich man claimed to have followed them all. But had he really? This man was rich; many in his country were poor. He had all the advantages: plenty of food to eat, a fine home, many servants, all that he needed plus much more. Many would have their sufferings alleviated if this man would give away his wealth to help them. He had it in his power to demonstrate his love for his neighbor by helping provide for their needs. He could only keep the commandment to love his neighbor by giving away his possessions.

Jesus challenged him to give up a selfish life and become generous. His possessions were used only for his own comfort. The only way to help the rich young man was to cut him loose from the grip of his wealth.

Jesus did not tell every wealthy man to give away all he had. If possessions were used as a means of helping others, they did not need to be disposed of.

We do not know what the rich young man did after he was confronted by Jesus.

The Problem of Wealth
Matthew 19:23-26

It is hard for the rich to enter the kingdom for several reasons: It makes this world more attractive and ties a person down to earthly concerns. It gives a person a sense of false independence by making him/her think he/she needs no help from God. Having much makes a person want more. After gaining more than enough to provide for essentials in life, the only satisfaction comes from acquiring more. Riches tend to make people selfish.

Jesus did not say it was impossible for the rich to enter the kingdom of God. Zacchaeus was one of the richest men in Jericho. Nicodemus was wealthy and so was Joseph of

Arimathaea. There is no hint that any of them gave away all they had.

The less a man has on this earth to worry about the more time he has for God's service.

The Reward of the Christian
Matthew 19:27-30

To say that Christians should never think about rewards is contrary to what Jesus said. Peter wanted to know what reward he was going to receive for giving up everything to be a disciple of Jesus. On the other hand, if we give our lives to Jesus Christ for the reward we will get out of it, we may be disappointed. We are not promised success or material wealth, or even a long life. But the reward we will receive if we have been faithful to God will be greater than we could ever imagine. The gifts God gives to us are more precious than any material blessing. The rewards may not be evident now but they will be eventually.

Those who think they are first in the kingdom may discover they will be last. Only God can make the final evaluation of our lives.

Parable of the Workers
Matthew 20:1-16

This parable describes an event that took place frequently in Palestine. The grape harvest comes at the end of September when the grapes are ripe. It has to be done quickly before the fall rains come which would ruin the crop.

The workers were hired at the beginning of the day to do a certain job at the wage of about twenty cents. This sounds very low by modern standards but it was enough to provide food for a family for one day. At nine o'clock the employer went out to the market place and told the workers standing around idle to go work in the vineyard and they would receive fair payment for their work. The same thing was done at noon and at 3:00. Then at 5:00 he once again went to the market place and told some more workers to go work in the vineyard.

When all the workers were called together to receive their pay, the men who worked only one hour received the same amount that was agreed upon by the men who had worked twelve hours. The all-day men thought they would receive a bonus but they too were paid one denarius. They protested that it was not fair. But the employer reminded them that they had made an agreement on the wage.

There are several lessons in the parable:

1) God does not reward us according to the number of deeds we have done. The first hour men worked solely for the pay and received the agreed upon amount. The last hour men worked because the opportunity was given to them. They had no thought of a reward. Yet they received a generous wage. We should serve the Lord only for the joy of serving.

2) God is generous to all. The employer knew that all the men needed enough money to buy food for their families or else they would go hungry. It was not the amount of service that was important but the attitude in which the service was done. All the men were given enough to provide for their families. God provides for all his children.

3) Some accept Jesus Christ early in life while others do not know him until late in years. This does not mean that those who have served God for many years have an advantage over those who have not. God does not keep a credit-debit ledger with a record of our good and bad deeds.

What God gives us is grace, i.e., a gift out of his goodness, not pay for service rendered. All are equally precious to God regardless of the length of time they have served him.

The Third Passion Prophecy
Matthew 20:17-19

Jesus again took his disciples to a place off the road and explained that he would be tried, condemned and put to death in Jerusalem. The disciples would forget his promise that he would rise again even though Jesus had repeated it several times.

A Mother's Ambition
Matthew 20:20-28

It is possible that James and John were close relatives of Jesus. This incident shows that the disciples did not understand much of what Jesus had been saying. They still looked upon work in terms of gain and prestige. They were a part of the inner circle who were with Jesus, the Son of God, most of the time, and they felt this entitled them to a special place with special privileges. In the other Gospels the brothers themselves ask the question. In Matthew it is the mother who asks.

They claim that they are willing to drink the cup (suffer martyrdom, just as Jesus will). But, as Jesus points out, their place in heaven is a decision that only God can make.

The other disciples were upset that the question was asked. They might have felt this way because they also wanted a special place in the Kingdom. Jesus reminds them that greatness in God's service does not mean superiority over others; it means helping others.

Jesus came not as a king who demanded that others do favors for him; he came to give his life so that those who believed in him would be free from the grip that sin had on them. (A ransom was paid to free a slave or one held in bondage. The giving of his life was the price Jesus would pay.)

Two Blind Men
Matthew 20:29-34

The two blind men called Jesus by the title, "Son of David." They saw Jesus as a potential military leader who would lead the army of Palestine to victory over Rome. Although they had a mistaken understanding of who Jesus was, they were still given their sight. The blind men had the faith that Jesus could heal them even though they were not sure who he really was.

Jesus Enters Jerusalem
Matthew 21:1-11

This marked the beginning of Jesus' last week on earth. Each of the Gospel writers devoted several chapters to Holy Week. The entry into Jerusalem was not made by chance; Jesus had prepared for it in advance. He was not going to slip secretly into the city as he had done before. Many people who had come for the annual Feast of the Passover knew he would be coming.

His entry would fulfill the prophecy of Zechariah 9:9 which stated that the king would enter on a donkey and its colt. As he entered the city, riding on the animal, people took off their outer clothing and laid them down in front of him; others cut branches off of the trees and laid them in front of him. The shout of "Hosanna," which means "save now," was heard. Many people asked the question, "Who is this?" Others answered saying, "This is the prophet, Jesus of Nazareth." They saw him only as a prophet, a representative of God, not as the Messiah. They did not yet understand who he was.

Driving Out the Sellers
Matthew 21:12-17

We often think of Jesus as always being gentle and non-violent. But this occasion called for firmness. It made Jesus angry that the Temple was being used for purposes of financial gain. The Temple had been built for the worship of God. Selling animals for sacrifice was a perversion of the purpose of the Temple. The merchants were selling sacrificial animals without blemish for extremely high prices. This brought in extra money. Also, the Temple tax had to be paid with certain kinds of coins; not just any kind of money was acceptable. So there were money-changers in the Temple precincts who were responsible for the proper exchange of money. In order to change the money, they charged a fee for making the transaction. They were cheating the people who had come to make sacrifices there.

Jesus continued to do what he had always done: he healed the people of their diseases.

The religious leaders were outraged when they heard the

children yelling, "Hosanna."

Jesus spent the night in a town just south of the city.

The Empty Fig Tree
Matthew 21:18-22

This appears to be a strange story. Why would Jesus want to wipe out a fig tree? This story is a parable which is acted out. Sometimes prophets in Old Testament times would act out their messages to the people.

The time of the year in which this took place was Spring. Fig trees do not produce ripe figs until June. Fig trees do not have fully grown leaves until the fruit is ripe. Apparently something was wrong with this particular tree because the leaves had come out too soon and there were no figs.

The withering of the fig tree was symbolic of the situation with God's chosen people. They had become empty; they were not producing that which they were meant to produce. Since Israel was not bearing fruit it would be uprooted by God. Israel had become useless.

The words about "faith" seem to be out of place. It is a restatement of what Matthew has written before (see 17:20). This is not to be taken literally, for no one could actually change geography by prayer. A "mountain" refers to barriers and problems in our lives which can be removed or overcome through trust in God.

An Attempt to Trap Jesus
Matthew 21:23-27

Jesus had become popular with the people. The leaders of the Jewish religion felt threatened by the attraction of Jesus. He was contradicting their sacred traditions, and people were accepting his criticisms of their petty rules and regulations. They were jealous of him; they hated him. They did not attack him openly, but instead, they attempted to make him say something which they could use against him.

The question was asked, "By what authority are you doing

these things?" Jesus answered with a question, "Where did John's authority to baptize come from?" If they had taken John's baptism seriously, they would have known who Jesus was. John had proclaimed that Jesus was greater than he, and that his baptism would be the baptism of the Holy Spirit of God, not merely of repentance. So they give the feeble reply, "We don't know."

Parable of Two Sons
Matthew 21:28-32

The son who said he would go to the vineyard to work and then did not represented the nation of Israel who said they would obey God, but did not. The second son is symbolic of the prostitutes, tax collectors and other undesirables who said that they would go their own way but later changed their minds and turned to a life of obedience and faith in God. These people believed Jesus, while the so-called religious people did not.

This parable also tells us we should practice what we say. Our words mean nothing if our actions do not correspond to what we speak.

Parable of the Landowner
Matthew 21:33-42

Ordinarily a parable has only one point. The details usually lead up to the central meaning of the parable. This one is different; the details have meaning also. The meaning of all the details is so clear that they do not need much explanation.

The servants sent to collect the product are the prophets of the Old Testament. They were rejected by the people; some were murdered. The son was Jesus Christ. He, too, would be rejected and killed by the people. Then the owner (God) would turn the responsibility of collecting the produce over to the other tenants (nations) who would obey the owner.

The stone which was rejected is Jesus himself, the most important person in the world. Those who regard Jesus Christ as not essential to their lives will discover in time that they have made a grave mistake.

The hatred of the chief priests and Pharisees was intensified when they realized that he was talking about them.

The Wedding Supper
Matthew 22:1-4

Here is another parable directed against God's chosen people who have rejected God's will. The invitations were sent out for the wedding feast, but the time for the occasion was not given. Finally, when the feast was ready the servants were sent out to tell the people to come. But the people were not interested. The king sent out some more servants, but this time the people became annoyed and killed the servants. The king was so furious that he destroyed their city.

The invitation was issued to Israel to serve God and enjoy his blessings. But down through history they refused. The servants were the prophets and the holy men who continually issued the invitation of God to be his people.

The people went too far by killing God's representatives, so their city was destroyed. The city was Jerusalem, which was leveled by Rome in 70 A.D. Matthew wrote his Gospel after the destruction of Jerusalem had occured; he was looking back, commenting on the reason why the sacred city had been destroyed. Rome had become tired of the many rebellions of the Jews, so they razed the holy city to teach them a hard lesson. If the people had listened to Jesus, the city might not have been destroyed.

Again, the servants were sent out, only this time they were to bring anyone to the banquet who was willing to come. This included the good and the bad alike; there were no qualifications. These people were surprised at the summons to come because they knew they didn't deserve it. It was by the grace of the king that the invitation was offered.

The second part of the parable is more difficult to understand. The clothing has a symbolic meaning. The king opened the party up to anyone who would come. Those invited from the streets should have been grateful for the unexpected invitation. They should have prepared themselves for the festive event. This man was not prepared; he came in clothes unsuitable for the event.

It means that since God gives us his grace we should respond by getting rid of the old life of separation from God and put on the new life which is appropriate for reconciliation to God. God invites the sinner to come to him, but the sinner cannot continue to be a sinner. He must give up the old habits and actions which have prevented him from having the right relationship to God. He must be clothed in a new attitude. Many are invited, but few respond with joy and gratitude.

Caesar and God
Matthew 22:15-22

The intention of the Pharisees was to force Jesus to make a statement that would get him into trouble with Rome. They sent along some Herodians, those who were close allies of Herod. Herod had received his position from Rome, ruling the territory of Judea. The question was composed to make Jesus take sides for or against Rome.

If he said that it was all right to pay taxes to Rome, then he would lose the favor of the people, because of their hostility towards the nation that controlled them. If he said that taxes should not be paid, then they could accuse him of sedition, and Rome could bring a charge against him.

Jesus' answer was, "Give to Caesar what belongs to him, and give to God what belongs to him." The Kingdom of God would not come by weapons or violence. Jesus recognized the world situation; it would be a hopeless endeavor to attempt a revolution against a super power like Rome. God's Kingdom is a realm involving our hearts and minds. God is in control of the world anyway. Rome could only require money and services from its people; God requires our complete obedience which we owe to him. God holds the ultimate destiny of all human life in his hands.

A Question About the Resurrection
Matthew 22:23-33

The Sadducees were the wealthy, aristocratic class among the Jews. They belonged to the ruling class; the chief priests were Sadducees. They did not share many of the beliefs of the Pharisees who accepted most all of what is contained in the Old Testament. The only Scripture that the Sadducees recognized was the Pentateuch, which is the first five books of the Bible. The resurrection was not mentioned in these books so the Sadducees denied that there was a resurrection of the dead. The resurrection of the dead is only mentioned twice in the entire Old Testament (Isaiah 26:19; Daniel 12:2). The question they asked of Jesus was meaningless if they did not believe in the resurrection.

Deuteronomy 25:5-10 says that the brother of one who has died must marry the widow. The first child of the marriage will assume the dead father's name. If he refuses to marry the widow there is an insulting ritual which he is forced to endure.

Jesus said that life would be completely different in heaven. Marriage would not be necessary. Then he went on to show that the Sadducees were even wrong about their own Scriptures, the first five books of the Old Testament. There is a text that implies that life does not cease after earthly death. Exodus 3:6 tells us that God said to Moses, "I am the God of your father, the God of Abraham, the God is Isaac, and the God of Jacob." God cannot be God of dead men; he is the God of the living. These men had died before God said this to Moses. We remember that Jesus appeared on the mountain with Moses and Elijah; these men were still alive even though they had lived on earth hundreds of years before the time of Jesus.

The Greatest Commandment
Matthew 22:34-40

Again the Pharisees attempted to trip up Jesus. They met together and chose an expert in the Law to ask him, "What is the greatest commandment in the Law?" The commandment Jesus quoted in answer to the question was not unfamiliar to the people. It was not even one of the Ten Commandments but was recited every day by the faithful Jews. The greatest commandment is found in Deuteronomy 6:5, "You must love the Lord your God with all your heart, with all your soul, and with all your strength." The second part of this commandment is found in Leviticus 19:18, "You must love your neighbor as yourself."

But who loves God in all these ways and who loves his neighbor as he should? We all ignore God; we fail to do his will; we sin against him. So each of us must depend on God's great mercy towards us. We love ourselves more than we do others, and we often offend them without even realizing it. It is only through our dependence on God that we find forgiveness from him.

We are commanded to love God and men. We are commanded to be devoted to our creator and to be of service to all people. These two commandments take precedence over any others contained in the Scriptures.

David's Son and Lord
Matthew 22:41-46

Jesus asked them a question, "What is your opinion about the Christ? Whose son is he?" They answered, "David's." It was believed that the Messiah would be a descendant of King David. Then Jesus asked them another question they could not answer. "Why is it that David called the Messiah his Lord?" This refers to a quotation taken from Psalm 110:1. The first "Lord" in this psalm is God, the second "Lord" is the Messiah. How could Christ (Messiah) be David's Lord and son at the same time? The answer is that the Son of God (Jesus Christ) has always existed with God.

The Gospel writer, John, reports the words of John the Baptist (John 1:15) regarding Jesus: "This is the one of whom I said, 'He who comes after me ranks before me because he existed before me.' " John was born before Jesus on earth, yet Jesus Christ existed before John the Baptist. It is not enough to call Jesus Christ the "son of David." He is the "Son of God." The questioning of the Pharisees and the Sadducees stopped.

Hypocrites
Matthew 23:1-12

Jesus said that not everything the scribes and Pharisees taught was to be ignored. As long as they taught what Moses had received from God, it was to be obeyed. But they had gone beyond God's Laws. They had invented countless rules and regulations based on the Law; this made religion an impossible burden. They had made religion depressing by imposing all kinds of restrictions on life. They condemned others for not obeying all of their foolish rules. For example, they defined "work," which was forbidden on the Sabbath by the fourth commandment, as lifting anything which weighed more than the weight of two dried figs. How could a mother carry her own child without breaking the Law? The rules they had invented had become ridiculous.

The scribes and Pharisees liked to show off. They wore little boxes on their foreheads and arms which contained certain Bible verses; these were called "phylacteries." All Jews wore tassels on their clothing; so did Jesus. But the religious leaders made them longer so that they could impress others. They wanted to be seen and respected. They liked to be called, "Rabbi," which means "great." The more famous rabbis were called, "Father."

A follower of Christ must serve others, not be served by them. The mark of a Christian is humility, because he knows he is completely dependent on God; he has no claim to greatness. His only authority is Jesus Christ.

The Seven Indictments
Matthew 23:13-32

1) The scribes and Pharisees had interpreted God's Law with such strictness and had laid down so many regulations that nobody could obey the Law. The scribes and Pharisees could not even obey it themselves.

2) They went many miles to make a convert and then misled him by teaching a perverted concept of religion.

3) The scribes had composed laws for the taking of oaths. If a man took an oath, it meant that he had to do what he had promised. He could swear by the gold but not by the Temple

itself. Obviously, the Temple was more important than the metal contained in it. The same applied to the altar: which was greater, the altar itself or the offering on it? The altar was greater.

4) A tithe is one-tenth of what a man possesses. It is to be dedicated to God. This extended to all the crops a person raises. A man could even tithe little plants grown for flavoring. The scribes and Pharisees had become more concerned with trivialities than they were with their relationship to other people. They strained gnats out of their wine so that they would not swallow a little insect, but they gulped down a camel. This expression was used to show how they had lost their sense of values.

5) A rule of the Pharisees said that they should clean the outside of the cups and plates as well as the inside. To fail to do this was to break the Law. It was their hearts that were unclean, filled with hatred and prejudice.

6) Tombs were whitewashed along the road so that no one would become unclean because they had touched them. Jesus compared the Pharisees to those clean tombs which contained death on the inside. A person who did not love God was only a dead individual who appeared to be alive.

7) The scribes and Pharisees built monuments to the prophets to honor them. They claimed that they would not have killed them if they had lived in the time of the prophets. But Jesus knew that they were going to kill another representative of God soon — Jesus himself.

Jerusalem Failed to Respond

Matthew 23:37-39

Jerusalem was the Holy City. Yet the people had rejected the word of God over and over again. Jesus had visited there many times but the people had refused to listen. Jesus longed for them to accept him and his message, but they had rejected it. Forty years later the city was destroyed by the Romans who had become irritated by the constant rebellion of the Jews.

The Temple
Matthew 24:1-2

Herod the Great had begun work on the Temple forty-six years before. It was a magnificent building with large dimensions, beautiful beyond description. The disciples were shocked to hear that this beautiful edifice would be destroyed.

No One Knows
Matthew 24:3-51

What follows in this chapter is the combining of the coming destruction of Jerusalem with a description of what is to come in the last days when Jesus returns.

The Ten Bridesmaids
Matthew 25:1-13

Wedding customs are much different in the Middle East. , wedding was a big event in the life of a town or village. The wedding celebration lasted for several days, usually a week. In preparation for the wedding, bridesmaids kept the bride company while they waited for the groom to make his appearance. He could come at any time, even in the middle of the night. The wedding party must be ready at all times, because the groom might show up when they least expected him. Five of the bridesmaids in this story let their lamps get low on oil, so they were forced to go out and buy more. In the meantime, the bridegroom arrived while they were out. They returned to find the door shut and locked.

This parable tells us that we must be prepared at anytime for the return of Jesus Christ. The foolish ones are those who have let their lights of faith die out. They are the ones who have stopped believing in God; therefore they have no access to God.

Parable of the Talents
Matthew 25:14-30

Not everyone has been given the same amount of abilities, responsibilities, or talents. Some have been given more, and more will be expected from them. The first two men in the story doubled their talents. (A talent is worth about $1000.) The third man was given less than the other two. But he buried it and returned it to the master with nothing gained or lost.

All gifts given to us by God are meant to be used. If they are used, they will bring a return; they will be productive. The reward for using them may be greater responsibilities.

The emphasis here is on the one who does nothing with his gift from God. He gives it back the way it was. This story was directed at the Pharisees who kept the Law the way it was. They believed that the right relationship to God was to not do what was forbidden and to do only what the Law allowed. In a sense they were obeying God by doing nothing.

This story also says that God intends for us to use our gifts in a productive way. We must use what we have been given to help others, to make a better community, or to make life better for people. We cannot keep God's gifts to ourselves; they must be shared with others.

The Final Judgment
Matthew 25:31-46

It will not be God the Father who judges us; that responsibility is given to Jesus Christ. This means that we cannot say that we believe in God alone; we must also make a decision about Jesus Christ.

The picture is of Jesus as a Shepherd separating sheep (the faithful) from the goats (the unbelievers). What will be the standard by which we will be judged? It will not be by the amount of knowledge we have absorbed, nor our theological comprehension. We will be judged by the help we have given to others. Our fame, success or wealth will not be considered.

Helping a person in need, helping a person to become better, or helping a person in trouble is like helping Jesus Christ. We must not turn anyone away.

The Plot Against Jesus
Matthew 26:1-5

Jesus finished his teaching; the time for his trial was only hours away. The religious leaders were together in the house of the chief priest making plans to arrest Jesus. Caiaphas was high priest at this time. He held this position for eighteen years.

Demonstration of Love
Matthew 26:6-13

Jesus and his disciples had spent some time at Bethany during his last week. Now Jesus was at the house of Simon whom he had probably healed of leprosy. A woman came and poured an expensive ointment on the head of Jesus. The disciples complained about this seeming waste. Mark tells us that the jar was worth over sixty dollars. A fair wage for one day's work was about twenty cents. The contents of the jar was worth a whole year's wages.

The concern of the disciples seemed justified; the sale of this ointment could have helped many poor people. We cannot be sure that this was their motive for complaining. They might have been thinking about the money and not the poor.

More important was the motive of the woman. She expressed her love and devotion by giving something of great value to Jesus. True love does not stop to calculate the cost. Love is freely given without considering the loss or waste. This was the best way she knew how to express her love for him.

Judas Makes a Bargain
Matthew 26:14-16

Judas requested money for turning Jesus over to the chief priests. The amount they offered him was thirty pieces of silver, the price for a slave. Judas would choose a time and place so that they could arrest Jesus without stirring up a crowd.

Why did Judas betray Jesus? There are several possibilities.

1) He was greedy and wanted money. John told us that he was a thief. But thirty pieces of silver was not much more than ten dollars. It would have been a poor bargain.

2) He hated Jesus. Jesus did not measure up to his idea of what Jesus should do. Judas wanted a great leader who would defy Rome by using great powers. Instead Jesus taught and practiced non-violence and gentleness.

3) He wanted to force Jesus' hand. He did not intend for Jesus to be killed. He wanted to force his master into a situation which would compel him to take action. Judas wanted to see Jesus defeat the opposition by a show of force. Judas wanted to see a showdown. When he realized that he had made a terrible mistake, he killed himself.

Preparations for Passover
Matthew 26:17-19

The Day of Unleavened Bread had been observed since the Israelites had been delivered from Egypt. They had left Egypt in such a hurry that they had no time to bake bread with leaven in it. Leaven was fermented dough which made the bread rise, giving it a good flavor. Unleavened bread is like a dry cracker which has a flat taste. Unleavened bread was symbolic of the slavery they had left behind. Leaven was also the symbol of rottenness and corruption. The lack of leaven symbolized purification.

On Thursday morning every piece of leaven was thrown out of the houses of the Jews. It was on this day that the disciples went to the owner of the house with the upper room; there they prepared for the Passover meal. Jesus had already made the arrangements.

Judas' Betrayal Is Known
Matthew 26:20-25

During the meal Jesus made a startling statement that one of the disciples was going to betray him. Judas must have kept his plans a well hidden secret because none of the other disciples had any idea it was he. Jesus had known that he must die; this was God's plan for salvation. He also knew that Judas would become disloyal. If he had known this from the beginning, why did Jesus call him as a disciple? Couldn't he have spared Judas his terrible fate if he had chosen someone else? Jesus would have met death eventually without the assistance of Judas. On the other hand, all of us betray our Lord at one time or another. We do it by not believing in his promises, or by not doing what we know is right. We are all in need of God's mercy. It is not our right or within our powers to judge others; we do not know the motives of others, and we do not know what was in the mind of Judas.

The Lord's Supper
Matthew 26:26-29

It was customary to give thanks before eating a meal. Jesus broke off pieces of the bread and gave it to each of the disciples. Jesus gave the bread a new meaning which has been sacred to Christians since then. The breaking of the bread was symbolic of his body. His body would be nailed to the cross, the most gruesome instrument of death known to man. He would be tortured and killed for the benefit of all who believed in him. The wine was symbolic of his blood which would fall from his body, signifying a new covenant with all believers. The old covenant was associated with Moses, who took the blood from an animal sacrifice and threw half of it on the altar and the other half on the people. This signified communion with God (he would be their God and they would be his people by obeying his commandments). The new covenant established communion with God (we have forgiveness of our sins and we are reconciled to God through faith).

It is unfortunate that Christians have used Holy Communion

as an occasion for division and exclusion down through the years.

Peter Will Deny Jesus
Matthew 26:30-35

Psalms were always sung to end the Passover feast. Another startling statement came from Jesus. He knew his disciples were weak; he knew they would not be able to stand up to the test. He told them that they would turn away from him. Again, he told them of his Resurrection which apparently they failed to believe. Then, Peter, true to form, made a bold statement that he alone would survive the trial of faith. But Jesus predicted that before the rooster crowed, he would have denied knowing him three times. After Peter made his boast the disciples made similar ones.

Jesus Prays in the Garden
Matthew 26:36-46

Jesus had many friends. One was a man who owned a garden; he allowed Jesus and his disciples to come there whenever they wished. Again, Jesus took his close circle of friends, Peter and his two cousins, James and John (the brothers were probably related to Jesus), into the garden. He asked them to stay awake while he prayed.

Jesus then prayed, "If it be possible, let this cup pass me by." The "cup" meant the "death he would have to endure." Jesus did not accept his coming death with a calm, detached attitude. He was deeply troubled; he was in terrible anguish; the weight of the sins of the world was on him. It was an awesome responsibility, and he was overcome by it. The thought of escaping death did not remain with him for long. He knew that God's will must be done. God had planned this and Jesus knew his Father would be with him during the whole experience. Because of this experience, Jesus is able to sympathize with our struggles and is able to give us strength to overcome them. The disciples could not keep awake; they fell asleep each time Jesus went off to pray. They seemed unconcerned.

Jesus Is Arrested
Matthew 26:47-56

It is strange that such a large armed force was required to arrest a man who had never practiced violence except in the Temple. Judas stepped forward and kissed Jesus. Here, Jesus called him "friend." Jesus still loved him and Judas could still be forgiven; he could still back out. John tells us that it was Peter who pulled out a sword and missed his mark, cutting off the ear of a servant.

To defend Jesus by violence was against everything he ever taught. The church through the ages has often forgotten this. It is still happening today in other parts of the world.

Jesus reminded them that the Scripture must be fulfilled. When the disciples saw that Jesus would not resist but would be arrested, they ran away.

The Trial
Matthew 26:57-68

The Sanhedrin was the highest court in Palestine. It was composed of seventy-one men: scribes, Pharisees, Sadducees and elders. A quorum for a meeting was twenty-three. There were rules governing the meetings. All criminal cases must be tried and completed during the daytime; Jesus was tried at night. Cases could not be tried during Passover; it was during the Passover that the trial took place. A guilty verdict could only be passed after one night had passed; this was not done. They could meet only in the Hall of Hewn Stone; they met at the house of the High Priest. It was necessary to have two witnesses separately interviewed; only lying witnesses could be found. It is easy to see how much they hated Jesus for they were willing to break so many of their own rules to get rid of him.

The witnesses claimed that Jesus had said that he would destroy the temple, which had taken forty-six years to build, and then would rebuild it in three days. He had predicted the destruction of the Temple, but he had never said that he would do it himself. They twisted his words to give what he had said a different meaning.

Jesus had used the term "temple" to describe his own body which would be put to death. "In three days build it up" meant the time in between his death and Resurrection.

Then the High Priest, Caiaphas, asked him if he was the Christ. If Jesus had said, "No," he could have walked out a free man. If he said, "Yes," they would have a charge against him. Jesus not only said that he was the Messiah, he quoted a passage from the book of Daniel with its account of the victory of God's Chosen One (Daniel 7:13). "And I saw, coming on the clouds of heaven, one like a Son of Man."

The way to express shock and anger was by the tearing of one's outer clothing. Jesus was accused of blasphemy, i.e., claiming to be equal with God.

Pandemonium followed; some spit on his face and some hit him in the face. This was an unusual way for members of a high court to conduct themselves.

Peter Lies

Matthew 26:69-75

Peter was not the coward the other disciples were. He was brave enough to follow the proceedings to the courtyard of the house of Caiaphas. But then someone recognized him. The servant girl had seen him with Jesus. Peter denied that he was ever with him. Another servant girl made the same observation and said it loud enough for all to hear. Again, Peter denied knowing Jesus, and this time he swore he did not know him. Another person identified him as one who was a disciple of Jesus, because of his Galilean accent. The accent was obvious. It was so offensive to some, that Galileans were not allowed to give the benediction at a religious service. Peter cursed louder than ever.

Then he heard the sound that he dreaded so much. The rooster crowed. All of a sudden his mind went back to the prediction of Jesus that he would do exactly as he had just done. Peter was overcome; he had failed again.

Jesus Is Taken to Pilate
Matthew 27:1-2

The Jews were allowed to pronounce verdicts in all cases except ones which involved the death sentence. That could only be done by the Romans. The Sanhedrin wanted his death so they sent him to Pilate. They needed a charge which would bring about the death penalty. Blasphemy would not do this since it was not offensive to Rome.

Only Luke tells us what charges were contrived that would result in a death sentence (23:2). He was charged with inciting a riot, refusing to pay taxes, and claiming to be a king.

Judas Kills Himself
Matthew 27:3-10

It appears as though Judas had expected Jesus to escape the death sentence. If Judas had wanted Jesus to die, he would have found satisfaction in the trial. He might have betrayed Jesus in order to force his hand and make him use violent means to overcome his enemies. Instead, Judas felt remorse; he took the money and threw it at the chief priests and elders. Then he went out and hanged himself. The money could not go into the treasury, so it was used to buy a graveyard.

Jesus Is Sentenced
Matthew 27:11-31

Pontius Pilate was governor of Judea for ten years. Pilate must have been impressed with Jesus, especially by his silence. He saw the chance to let Jesus go because of a custom which allowed the release of a political prisoner during a festival. He was sure that the crowd would prefer Jesus of Nazareth over Jesus Barabbas. Only Matthew tells about the dream of Pilate's wife which had warned her that her husband should leave Jesus alone.

The crowd shouted for Barabbas' release. Was this the same crowd that shouted "Hosanna" in the streets of Jerusalem a few days before? There were thousands of people in Jerusalem during the week. They had come from many countries for the great Feast of the Passover. No doubt this was a different crowd which shouted for Jesus' crucifixion.

Pilate used the custom of washing his hands to rid himself of the guilt of not having stood up for his convictions. He had rid himself of the responsibility of Jesus' death, or had he? Pilate is remembered as a coward who let others decide what he knew was wrong.

Jesus Is Ridiculed
Matthew 27:27-31

A person condemned to die was first beaten before he was crucified. The soldiers added further insult by dressing Jesus up like a king. They were making fun of the Jewish idea of a king-like Messiah. Jesus was accused of claiming to be a king. This was one of the charges which could bring the death penalty. Then Jesus was led off to be executed.

The Crucifixion
Matthew 27:32-38

A man who was to be crucified was required to carry his own cross. After the beating, Jesus was so weak he could not do it, so a man nearby was ordered to carry the cross. When they arrived at Golgotha, the soldiers gave him a drink to take away the pain, but Jesus refused to take it. He did not want his mind altered; he would not allow the pain to be lessened. He was suffering for the sins of the world and he would take their full force.

The soldiers were familiar with crucifixions, so much so that they were indifferent to all the agony above them. They even gambled for his clothing because they had nothing more to do than guard the area.

The sign above his head displayed the charge that brought the death sentence: "This is Jesus, the King of the Jews."

Jesus was crucified between two thieves. Matthew does not tell us about the conversation of the thieves with Jesus.

Jesus Is Mocked
Matthew 27:39-44

Again, the people used the words that Jesus had said and twisted them to mean something other than what was intended. Jesus did not say he would destroy the Temple and afterwards reconstruct it. He was referring to himself in symbolic language. "If he is all he claims to be," they said, "then he can come down off the cross." Because he did not save himself, he showed himself to be the obedient Son of God. Jesus had it within his power to do so. He overcame the last temptation just as he had overcome other temptations.

The Death of Jesus
Matthew 27:45-55

Darkness spread all over the country from noon to three o'clock in the afternoon. And then Jesus cried out, "My God, my God, why have you deserted me?" This is the opening phrase of Psalm 22 which concludes with an affirmation of trust in God. Some thought that Jesus was crying out for Elijah the prophet because the first two words of the psalm in Hebrew sound like the name "Elijah."

With a loud cry Jesus died on the cross.

The Temple curtain was split in two. This was the entrance to the Holy of Holies in which only the High Priest could enter on the Day of Atonement. Only on that day could God's name be said out loud, and then only by the High Priest. No longer was God hidden to people. Now, all could have direct access to God through Jesus Christ. God's ways were no longer a secret; Jesus had shown men and women what God is like.

The tombs were opened and dead men came to life, demonstrating that Jesus had overcome death.

It was a centurion who perceived that Jesus was from God. Three other centurions in the New Testament made similar affirmations.

It was the women who remained close to Jesus. The disciples had run away. The women went unnoticed because they held such a low position in society.

Jesus Is Placed in a Tomb
Matthew 27:57-61

The relatives and disciples of Jesus were in no position to take Jesus' body to a tomb. They were from Galilee; the crucifixion took place in Judea. The Law said that a body must be buried the same day as the day of death. If a body was not claimed, it was left to rot. Joseph was a wealthy man and owned a tomb in the area.

Preventive Measures
Matthew 27:62-66

The Jewish leaders feared that Jesus might actually do what he said he was going to do, i.e., rise from the dead. To prevent this, they requested Pilate to post a guard and seal the stone at the entrance of the tomb. They made the request on the Sabbath, thereby breaking another law. They also feared that the disciples might attempt to steal his body and then circulate the story that Jesus had been raised from the dead.

The Empty Tomb
Matthew 28:1-10

These two women had been present at the crucifixion. They were the first ones to know about the Resurrection. The scene is electrifying: the earth shook; the angel's appearance shocked and paralyzed the guards; the women were fearful and joyful. They were the ones who would inform the disciples of the Resurrection. Apparently, the disciples did not believe that Jesus would be raised on the third day: why were the disciples not near the tomb waiting for Jesus to emerge?

The Bribe
Matthew 28:11-15

The soldiers returned with their version of what had

happened. The last resort was to bribe the soldiers with a lot of money, claiming that Jesus' friends stole the body during the night. Who would believe this? How could the guards have slept while a large stone was being removed? There would have been a loud commotion that would have surely alerted the soldiers.

The Commission
Matthew 28:16-20

We recall that after Peter had confessed that Jesus was the Christ at Caesarea Philippi, Jesus began to talk of his coming death and Resurrection. We can assume that the disciples did not really believe this would take place, because of their subsequent behavior. Even after seeing Jesus on the mountain, some were still not convinced it was true.

Jesus assured them that because he had been raised from the dead, they would be able to go anywhere on the face of the earth with the message that he had entrusted to them. They would know that Jesus would accompany them in their travels and experiences until he returned. Their purpose would be to bring others under the rule of Jesus Christ, initiating them into that company of believers by baptism in the name of the Father, Son and Holy Spirit.